BRUCE OLIVER

SENSATIONAL CUBA
Read, Plan, Visit, & Cook:
with tidbits, stories and ethnic recipes

– A Non-Scratch N Sniff Edition –

Discover the World, Travel & Cook
A Sensational Travel & Food Resource Series™
SensationalTravelBooks.com
Traveling Coloring Books Series™
TravelingColoringBooks.com

With Bruce Oliver, Luxury Travel Host
Host of: BruceOliverTV.com – Smart TV Travel & Food Network

Axis Mundi Systems LLC dba Cruise with Bruce Enterprises

Copyright © 2017 by Bruce Oliver - Travel Advisor & TV Host
Published by Vegas New Wave Media

The photograph used on the front and back covers, is courtesy of: Liv Otterk and her Amateur Travel Photography Blog located at: https://happywanderer15.wordpress.com. She said that:

"It is a picture of the spices for sale at the Grand Bazaar in Istanbul, Turkey. Again, the Bazaar is a great place to shop for tourists, but it's not super touristy. The vendors are friendly, and it's a great environment to walk around in. If you want more information look at the other post about spices"

Printed in the United States of America.

ISBN-13: 9781970029031

DEDICATION

To my traveling companions during my visit to Cuba.
My cousin and her husband…
Ron and Carol Lodder

CONTENTS

ACKNOWLEDGMENTS

I have many people to thank for help in producing this book.

I addition I'd like to thank my mom (Liz Oliver, Senior Editor in Chief) for being a sounding board. Her help caused me to make additions and changes as I went through the process to end up with what I present to you as the final product. I also thank many friends and family members that offered their advice from time to time.

I give a special thanks to Ignacio Maza at Signature Travel Network, who allowed me to use some of the material from his blog.

Special thanks go out to two fellow travel professionals Eva Holguin and Linda Oster-Safier for allowing me to use a couple of their photographs in my book.

TRAVELING IS GOOD FOR YOUR HEALTH!

As a youth, I listened to my elders say, over and over, that the one thing they wish they had done more often was take longer vacations when they had their young families. Seldom did someone say I wish I had worked more. Couples who wait until retirement to travel may have lost their opportunity to travel while they were together or in good health. Now, one woman said, he's passed and it's too late. Another said, "When we were young we thought that we'd be healthy forever. But now I must go for dialysis and it's too late! (Not really, many cruise lines can accommodate people on dialysis.)

My father relayed the same information to me as his health was failing just before his death. The prior year, for the first time in his life, he and mom went with my brother, sister, her son, my aunt and uncle and I on a two-week vacation to Edinburg, Scotland and London, England. He said that he wished he had more time to go again but it was too late for him, "not for you" he said, "Now I understand why you always travel." People nearing the end of life always say they wish that they took more time to "smell the roses".

I love everything about travel. Early in life I always made time to go somewhere new. Maybe it was because I belonged to a Scout Troop that always took us on vacations to Washington, D.C., World's Fairs in Montreal and New York City or destinations that the average boy would never visit. As an Eagle Scout, I was awarded a 30-day bus trip across the United States to hike for twelve days at Philmont National Boy Scout Reservation in Cimarron, NM. Today, I plan and use my vacations because I tend to be a workaholic. I plan a two-week vacation at least once per year and each quarter I have weekend trips to look forward to. This is especially important when things get difficult. Life is a sine wave with ups and downs. When the down periods come I always say, but I'm going on a cruise in a few weeks. Knowing this helps me cope with the downs and I am more productive.

As a matter of fact, productivity experts have discovered that the longer it is between vacations: "Fatigue sets in, rigidity applies, and all creativity and innovation are lost — both of which need time away for other activities to increase the probability of new ideas," said Lotte Bailyn, an MIT researcher and author of the book "Breaking the Mold: Redesigning Work for Productive and Satisfying Lives. (Bailyn, 2006)" "Unhealthy overwork costs company's money for healthcare and creates stressful and unrewarding lives, both of which detract from the good work they are supposed to be furthering."

Everything that I've read says the same thing. The more and longer vacations that you take, the more productive you will be when you get back to work. I feel best coming back from a two-week vacation (I don't mean visiting relatives to paint their house either.) It usually takes me 3-4 days to begin to relax and the balance of the vacation is full of rest and relaxation. I've gotten to the point that the only time I say I'm on vacation is when I leave the country and get away from the phone which I answer 24/7 and my normal regiment.

According to Ellen Galinsky, President of Families and Work Institute, the longer your vacation, the less stress you'll feel. People's stress levels dropped significantly when they took over 6-days and more as they approached 13 or more consecutive days away from work and their regular routine life. Families participating in these vacations tend to be less depressed and form tighter bonds with other family members (Ellen Galinski, 2014). It's true, my siblings and I often talk about the time we spent camping each summer at Lake Ossipee in New Hampshire or at Clinton Beach in Connecticut.

Galinski says: "Knowing that skipping vacation stifles creativity, creates health problems, leads to stress, depression, and less-than-ideal home lives, it seems as if companies would make vacation enforcement a priority. But with a few exceptions, the experts say that is not happening. Vacation skipping is a topic that's often swept under the keyboard."

Both women and men alike benefit by taking vacations. After their study, Gump, PhD, MPH, and; Matthews, PhD at the American Psychosomatic Society, concluded: "The frequency of annual vacations by middle-aged men at high risk for coronary heart disease (CHD) is associated with a reduced risk of all-cause mortality and, more specifically, mortality attributed to CHD. Vacationing may be good for your health." (Gump & Matthews, 2000)

This reminds me of an email I received many long years ago. It was titled:

1000 Marbles

"The older I get, the more I enjoy Saturday mornings. Perhaps it's the quiet solitude that comes with being the first to rise, or maybe it's the unbound joy of not having to be at work. Either way, the first few hours of the Saturday morning are the most enjoyable.

A few weeks ago, I was shuffling towards the kitchen with a steaming cup of coffee in one hand and the morning paper in the other. What began as a typical Saturday morning turned into one of those lessons that life seems to hand you from time to time. Let me tell you about it.

I turned the volume up the on my radio to listen to a Saturday morning talk show. I heard an older sounding chap with the golden voice. You know the kind, he sounded like he should be in the broadcasting business himself.

He was talking about "a thousand marbles" to someone named "Tom". I was intrigued and sat down to listen to what he had to say.

"Well, Tom, it sure sounds like you're busy with your job. I'm sure they pay you well but it's a shame you must be away from your home and family so much. Hard to believe a young fellow should have to work 60 or 70 hours a week to make ends meet. Too bad you missed your daughter's dance recital."

He continued, "Let me tell you something Tom, something it has helped me keep a good perspective on my own priorities."

And that's when he began to explain his theory of "a thousand marbles." "You see, I sat down one day and did a little arithmetic. The average person lives about 75 years. I know, some live more and some live less, but on average, folks live about 75 years."

"Now then, I multiplied 75 times 52 and came up with 3,900 which is the number of Saturdays that the average person has in their entire lifetime. Now stick with me Tom, I'm getting to the important part."

"It took me until I was 55 years old to think about all of this in any detail," he went on, "and by that time I had lived through over twenty-eight hundred Saturdays. I got to thinking that if I lived to be 75, I only had about 1,000 of them left to enjoy."

"So, I went into a toy store and bought every single marble they had. I end up having to visit three toy stores to round up 1000 marbles. I took them home and put them inside a large clear plastic container right here on my workshop table next to the radio. Every Saturday since then, I've taken one marble out and threw it away."

"I found that watching the marbles diminish caused me to focus more on the really important things in life. There's nothing like watching your time here on this earth run out, to help get your priorities straight."

"Now let me tell you one last thing before I sign-off with you and take my lovely wife out for breakfast. This morning, I took the very last marble out of the container. I figure if I can make until next Saturday then God has blessed me with a little extra time to be with my loved ones..."

"It was nice to talk to you Tom, I hope you spend more time with your loved ones, and I hope to meet you again someday. Have a good morning!"

You could have heard a pin drop when he hung up the phone. Even the shows moderator didn't have a thing to say for a few moments. I guess he gave us all a lot to think about.

I had planned to do some work that morning, then go to the gym. Instead, I went upstairs and woke up my wife with a kiss.

"C'mon Honey, I'm taking you and the kids to breakfast."

"What brought this on?" she asked with a smile. "Oh, nothing special," I said. "It has just been a long time since we'd spent Saturday together with the kids. Hey, can we stop at the toy store while we're out? I need to buy some marbles."

Have a great weekend and may all Saturdays be special and may your happy years continue long after you lose all your marbles."

INTERACTIVE VERSION

This book is available online, Kindle, NOOK, iPad, Smartphones, and in print. The interactive version has video, audio and additional information about the recipes, techniques, ideas trivia and other fun things to add to the experience. You can get this information on the computer, the internet, iPad, Android device, Blackberry and your smart devices.

The customer can also register for additional services. Product discounts and other value-added promotions. Pages with this iPad image or the BruceOliverTV logo indicates there is additional information online. The fee to access the channel full with video information and more can be accessed for a nominal monthly fee.

http://SmartTVtraveler.com

http://Promotions.CruiseWithBruce.com

READ

Introduction

Like most baby boomers, I heard about Cuba in grade school when I was 10 years old. After the Bay of Pigs invasion and rebellion by the citizens of Cuba, Fidel and Raul Castro got a grip on the entire country that they maintain until this day. President John F. Kennedy placed an embargo on the 780-mile Cuban island that is just 90 miles south of the Florida Keys after the Russians started moving nuclear missiles around the island of Cuba. (NSA | CSS - Cuban Missile Crisis, 1960-64) (NSA Archives, 1962).

My memories of that time included our weekly "get under your desk drills just in a case of nuclear attack". Well that was over 45 years ago, and today the citizens in the United States are joining the Canadians and British as we look at tourism in Cuba.

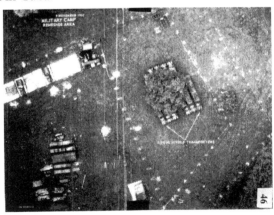

0-1 Nuclear Warheads in Cuba

Image 0-1 is from the CIA briefing board for JFK showing range of Soviet MRBMs (Bobby Kennedy on 16 October jokingly asked whether the missiles could hit Oxford, Mississippi, where federal marshals had intervened only two weeks earlier, so Oxford was included). PSALM was the special code word for intelligence data on missiles in Cuba, a compartment created at President Kennedy's insistence for greater control of this sensitive information.

0-2 Map of potential nuclear destruction

(Range of Cuban Missiles, 1962) (The National Security Archive, 1962)

Image 0-2 was taken November 9, 1962: Low-level photograph of 6 Frog (Luna) missile transporters under a tree at a military camp near Remedios. U.S. photo analysts first spotted these tactical nuclear-capable missiles on October 25, but only in 1992 did U.S. policymakers learn that nuclear warheads for the Lunas were already in Cuba in October 1962

This travel and food resource guide is for people traveling to Cuba from the United States. Since Fidel Castro's death and the election of President Donald Trump in November of 2016 the political scenery is changing and will continue to change for the foreseeable future. Most tour guides currently on the market are written for people that travel from other countries around the world to Cuba. It is important to note that hotels, restaurants and small businesses in

Cuba's severe economic downturn in 1990 followed the withdrawal of Soviet annual subsidies worth $4-6 billion. My guides echoed the views of the Cuban government as they blamed all of their problems on Kennedy's embargo in 1961.

this book may or may not exist in the future. This is true for international resorts and hotels currently there or may be built in the next few years. Everything is changing in Cuba. Raul Castro's attitude is more favorable towards travel for the Cuban economy than was Fidel's. Travelers from United States and the relaxation of the embargo by the U.S. Department of Treasury and the Federal Government stand to create a better relationship between the two countries. It will take another 10 to 15 years for the Cuban government to upgrade and build hotels to accommodate all the visitors and that want to visit their country. Outside of a couple of international resorts most of the major hotels and restaurants are owned by the Cuban government.

For over 20 years the Canadians followed by the British have been the most active visitors to Cuba. Cuba is the seventh largest island in the world and the largest island in the Caribbean. The beaches are beautiful, the people are wonderful, and the culture has not changed significantly in the last 40 to 50 years. U.S. visitors to the Cuban Island started with academic and medical visitations as well as those from journalism. In the last few months the regulations regarding the visit of American citizens to Cuba have been relaxed.

Starting the fall of 2015, over 20,000 U.S. citizens joined the people-to-people tours to see the wonderful nation and people of Cuba. But things are still somewhat up in the air since the United States government and the Cuban government have many regulations regarding visits of the average citizen from the United States to the island of Cuba. In 2016, tours by several approved tour operators and cruise lines have started visiting the island. To date most tours are either sold out or selling out quickly.

The purpose of the trip to Cuba is regulated by both governments agencies and rules. Someone visiting the island can expect to go back in time to the 1950s in the 1960s. This means that the island does not have many of the amenities and comforts that the average citizen is used to when they travel in the United States and the rest of the world. The tourism industry is still developing and accommodations on land are being overtaxed and booked solid. There's only so much that the people of this friendly country can

> Admiral Christopher Columbus is known as Admiral Cristóbal Colón; the Cristóbal Colón Cemetary was commissioned in Havana.

do especially when it comes to infrastructure that delivers hot water, ample supplies of flour, and transportation that we're used to in the United States. My friend says you need to bring your sense of humor.

You can expect to find out all about the culture of this country, its food, music, historic sites, and people. Because this country is so large you should not expect to see more than 2 to 4 major cities on the island. This is due to the transportation available in the expansive island that is as big as the state of Pennsylvania in square miles. Most people spend a large part of their time in Old Havana and greater Havana. Other centers that are visited in a seven-day period by U.S. Visitors are Cienfuegos and Trinidad, as well as Santiago de Cuba.

Cuba Facts

Background

Cuba is a tropical island slightly smaller than Pennsylvania with a population of just over 11 million people; it's one of the Caribbean's most visited islands. Home to beautiful mountain ranges and gentle plains, the island has more than 200 bays and nearly 300 beaches. Temperature ranges from a high of roughly 86 degrees Fahrenheit in July to a low of 70 degrees Fahrenheit in January,

In 1492, Christopher Columbus discovered Cuba landing in a place he named Porto Santo, some say it is one of two cities Baracoa or Gibraltar. Columbus also described a nearby Table Mountain that most people believe is El Yunque. In his log book he said that it the most beautiful place in the world; the birds sing that they will never ever leave. During his first landing he erected a cross "Cruz de la Parra" on the beach of Baracoa harbor. Over the next couple of centuries Cuba was a Spanish colony up until the Spanish-American War in 1898. At that time U.S. government led by the leader of the "rough riders" helped Cuba gain its independence from Spain. It was interesting to note that our guide referred to the conflict as the "Cuban Spanish American War" as we toured the sight of the battle of San Juan Hill in Santiago de Cuba.

Our guide referred to the Spanish American War as the "Cuban Spanish American War"

Before the war, the Spanish brought large numbers of African slaves to work the coffee and sugar plantations. Havana became a major port for ships going to Spain from Mexico and Peru. After the Spanish-American War and

the signing of the Treaty of Paris, Cuba gained its independence from Spain in 1898. For the next three-and-a-half years Cuba was under control of the US military. Finally, in 1902, Cuba became an independent republic under the control of a series of military and corrupt governments. In 1959, Fidel Castro over threw the corrupt government of

0-3 Sones y Boleros de Cuba played "Sexteto Emanuel"

Fulgencio Batista. Since 1959, Fidel Castro and his younger brother Raul Castro (after February 2008) named themselves President of Cuba and ruled with a tight fist all the way up to this day. I believe that their authoritarian rule is as bad as any of the regimes that ruled the island since 1902. Cuba's communist revolution, with Soviet support, was exported throughout Latin America and Africa during the 1960s, 1970s, and 1980s. The island is one of the last communistic nations in the Western Hemisphere.

After the revolution, Fidel Castro nationalized Catholic Churches and made them into museums or offices for the government. Santeria (Also known as La Regla Lucumi and the Rule of Osha.) replaced the church with a blend of African voodoo, combining the worship of traditional Yoruban deities with the worship of Roman Catholic saints. The syncretic religion was influenced by the slave trade in Cuba. People practicing Santeria are dressed in all white for the first year after joining. After a year women wear a red turban.

Cuba is the largest island in the Caribbean and the least developed therefore it has become a draw for many who want to avoid the bustling tourist traps of the Caribbean. Due to its proximity to the U.S., many believe Cuba will become a crowded tourist destination for Americans as travel restrictions loosen further. Tourists visiting the island experience a Cuba that is drastically different than the average Cuban lives in day to day. My group of journalists ate at the best government run restaurants and paladars on the island. We were shown the best side of Cuba. I had to dig to find out how the average Cuban Citizen lives. After the revolution and the trade embargo in 1961, tourists visiting Cuba from the United dropped to zero. As far as Fidel Castro was concerned that was fine because he linked tourism to criminals from the west. Everything changed after 1982 because the nation was cash poor and looked to an influx of cash into the Cuban economy from Europe and

Canada tourists. The Cuban government began to welcome foreign investment and building of resorts and hotels for tourists that wanted to visit the island. In the last six years, buildings built by Hilton and other hotel chains were confiscated and nationalized (Placed under the control of the Cuban Government).

When people think about Cuba they think about the country's love of lively music, (the mambo and salsa), fine cigar's and cocktails like the mojito. People from Chinese, Spanish and African cultures have joined the indigenous Tainos making Cuba an interesting place to visit. This diverse group of people have influenced everything from Cuba's cuisine to its music and secular religion (Santeria).

While Cuba is a fascinating tourist destination, not all aspects of life are rosy on this island paradise. Food shortages are still common, as are lines to get food when it is available. The economy suffered a difficult recession in 1990 with the collapse of the Soviet Union. At that time the leaders in their wisdom announced that the people were entering a "special period" where everyone would have to tighten their belts. That period has not ended and the Cuban infrastructure has continued to deteriorate. The Castro-led government and citizens blame the

In 2017, U.S. diplomats as well as tourists staying in hotels started experiencing problems with their hearing problems. Many believe that the Cuban Government is using high frequency sounds that caused the hearing loss.

U.S. trade embargo for many of the country's problems. Few citizens recall why the embargo was put in place by President John F Kennedy in the 1960's.

Others cite government control over the press and repression of those who oppose the Castro regime.

While many tourist destinations have their drawbacks, Cuba as a country still has much to offer tourists. Many travelers do choose to stay in luxury hotels or resorts owned by the Cuban regime, mostly run by European companies. And the many positive anecdotes from visitors to Cuba suggest that travelers do not

experience any of the hardships - in fact many raves about the overall experience.

What are the main attractions?

Cuba has a wide variety of attractions, sights and activities for tourists. The island's beaches are popular for European and Canadian visitors but U.S. Citizens are prohibited from vacationing on the island's beaches unless they go as part of the "People to People". Since 2014, guidelines have been put in place by agreement of the Cuban Government and the United States Department of Treasury.

History buffs will enjoy the feel that they've stepped back in time because there are relatively few new buildings in Havana. During my visit, I felt like I was visiting a Hollywood set where the fronts of the façades were newly painted but around the corner you could see that the buildings were in terrible shape.

Most of the cars are a real blast from the past and American "muscle cars" from the 1950s can be still seen all over Greater Havana. Havana also offers a wide variety of restaurants with local fare and nightclubs to experience the vibrant sounds of Cuba.

0-4 Havana Art Village building

Other common attractions include cigar tours to see how the world's finest are made, Ernest Hemingway-themed tours, eco-tours, scuba diving, fishing and golfing. Many travelers also go under the auspices of a religious or humanitarian organization and engage in social activities through their groups.

Is Cuba Economical?

Cuba is one of the more affordable destinations in the Caribbean, contrary to popular belief it is not a completely inexpensive location. Western resorts and hotels can even be expensive because the government gets a big cut. State-run hotels are modest in cost, as are stays at a private residence. Meals for foreign tourists or in the European hotels aren't a bargain either. Public transportation is cheap, but rental cars typically run higher than Florida. The best way to plan your trip safely, and cost-effectively is to talk to a travel agent specializing in Cuba who can steer you clear of both the tourist traps and the dumps.

> Why are paper bands on cigars? Several reasons have been cited. The one I like the best is about Catherine the Great in Russia, she had decorated silk bands put on her cigars so that her fingers wouldn't get stained. Today, paper bands are still prevalent.

While there are some obstacles that make travel to Cuba more challenging than most destinations, most who visit agree that the extra effort is more than worth it. Cuba is not a travel spot for everyone. Those interested in learning more and perhaps planning a trip to Cuba can contact me and I will assist you.

The Cuban Flag

The flag has five equal horizontal bands of blue (top, center, and bottom) alternating with white: a red equilateral triangle based on the hoist side bears a white, five-pointed star in the center; the blue bands refer to the three old divisions of the island: central, occidental, and oriental; the white bands describe the purity of the independence ideal; the triangle symbolizes liberty, equality, and fraternity, while the red color stands for the bloodshed in the independence struggle; the white star, called La Estrella Solitaria (the Lone Star) lights the way to freedom and was taken from the flag of Texas note: design similar to the Puerto Rican flag, with the colors of the bands and triangle reversed. (CIA Library, 2017)

U.S. Citizen Travel to Cuba

Since I started writing this book a few months ago many things have changed in Cuba and its relationship with the United States government and the people United States. Currently, Cuba is not a destination for U.S. Citizens to go to bask in the sun on one of Cuba's beautiful beaches as you might in the balance of the Caribbean. In 2014, there were all types of regulations written and agreed to by the United States Department of Treasury and the Cuban government (Fidel and Raul Castro). In the fall of 2016, the regulations changed once again before and may again after the death of Fidel Castro. It's very difficult to determine what regulations you, as a traveler to the island of Cuba will have to follow in the future. Therefore, I have the following link with the regulations on U.S. Department of Treasury site   https://www.treasury.gov/resource-center/sanctions/Programs/Pages/cuba.aspx.

Per the guidelines of the Department of Treasury (Disclaimer: Please note that this document serves for information purposes only and in no way claims to include all legal requirements):

"Nearly all sanctioned leisure travel to Cuba is provided under the guise of "people-to-people" exchange.

These are highly structured itineraries focusing on educational activities, including interactions with Cuba's musicians, artists, naturalists and entrepreneurs. All tour itineraries need to be preapproved by the United States Office of Foreign Asset Control (OFAC), and leave very little, if any, free time for the traveler to explore on their own. This means that the concept of truly independent travel to Cuba does not yet exist.

US citizens can legally travel to Cuba unaccompanied (meaning, on their own - not through a tour operator or DMC), but it is then the travelers' responsibility to ensure that all paperwork is executed properly, and that all sightseeing and activities comply with the "people-to-people" designation from OFAC. There are legal ramifications for the traveler if the itinerary does not comply, and all paperwork, including a general written record of each day's activities in Cuba as to the various sites visited and transactions or activities engaged in, must be kept for a minimum of five (5) years. We do not recommend this approach to visiting Cuba.

Recently, the US Treasury Department, which oversees OFAC, allowed US citizens to visit Cuban beaches as part of a people-to-people itinerary. In the past, it was argued that US citizens could not engage in substantive dialogue and activity with the citizens of Cuba while at a beach destination."

Currently there are 11 preferred land operators and 4 preferred cruise partners serving Cuba. And US Citizens are only allowed to travel to Cuba if their reason(s) for travel can be categorized in one of the following designated sections:

- Athletic and Other Competitions, Clinics, Exhibitions, Public Performances, and Workshops
- Educational Activities
- Family Visits
- Humanitarian Projects
- Journalistic Activities
- Official Government Business
- Professional Research and Professional Meetings
- Religious Activities
- Support for the Cuban People (often referred to as "people-to-people exchange")
- Activities of Private Foundations, Research, or Educational Institutes

For further information regarding these designated sections, please refer to the, (Department of Treasury, Office of Foreign Assets Control, Cuban Assets Control Regulations, 2016) (Legal Travel to Cuba, 2017)

Because of the complicated regulations and requirements by both governments I would recommend that you use a qualified agent to provide help to plan your vacation.

Arrival and Departure Advice

Prior to my visit to Cuba I applied for a visa and paid a $75 fee. I arrived in Cuba on a ship from Miami Florida. As I disembarked the ship in Havana the Cuban Government required me to have my Cuban Visa and U.S. Passport. The port authority removed the entry visa and stamped the exit visa. Each time I visited a different port I had to show the stamped visa and my U.S. Passport. If you fly into the country you will get half of the stamped visa back. In all cases you need to provide the stamped copy of the visa back before you fly out.

Upon departure, whether it be from your last port or airport, you will be required to surrender the stamped visa and pay a 25CUC departure tax. I would also like to note that you will also be required to pay a 25% tax, in CUCs, on artwork purchased in Cuba. If you do not have the proper number of CUCs to pay the tax then they will confiscate the piece or pieces of art that you purchased. Be sure to keep receipts for all artwork that you purchase to set the price that you paid or they will place a value on the art.

> **NOTE:** Unlike the border control in the United States the people in Cuba were all business. Photography and idle chatter are frowned upon and they were all business.

I suggest that you check into the airport, on departure, 3 hours prior to your flight's departure time. Many charter flights to the US run on an irregular schedule and your departure may actually depart an hour prior the posted time.

What to Bring

My friend Ignacio Mazza says you need to be very patient and flexible. Although the Cuba people are very open, friendly and outgoing they have little or no control over the service that you receive. Don't expect the same level of service that you expect at hotels and restaurants in the United States and Europe.

Due to over 50 years of socialism much of the infrastructure is in terrible shape. If you are on a land or ship tour the buses used for tourism are generally in good repair. But the streets in the country are cobblestone (especially Old Havana) and sidewalks are in poor shape therefore you should bring comfortable shoes.

Traveling in Cuba from June to September can be very warm and humid. Be sure to bring a hat and plenty of sun screen. I'd suggest that you bring sun screen to apply to sensitive areas year around.

If you have diet restrictions then traveling to Cuba can pose a problem. The proprietors of government and private restaurants will try to accommodate you but vegetarians may not have many options. Bring power bars or other food to tide you over if you are not fed on schedule.

Travel Insurance

Please contact your travel consultant to speak about available travel insurance protection.

Health and Safety

Health

As we traveled around Cuba I noticed one thing outside of the area frequented by the elite class. Depending upon the location water is provided through cisterns (roof top containers built to catch and store rainwater, photo on right) and the Cuban Citizens are limited to the number of hours that they can use the water (7:30 to 8:30 AM, 12 noon to

0-5 The cistern on the roof above provides water to the home through the black pipes.

0-6 Look at the grey and blue cisterns on the roof in Ceinfuegos.)

1:30 PM and 5:30 to 7 PM). When asked about their sanitation system my government guide would not answer the question.

As with other third world countries you should NEVER drink water that isn't bottled in Cuba. "That includes ICE!" That means you shouldn't use tap water to brush your teeth. Only drink bottled water that you can buy from a ship or luxury hotel. Only buy Ciego Montero mineral water (from a local spring, either flat or sparkling) which may cost up to 5CUCs or 5 U.S. Dollars. Avoid eating fresh salads, unpeeled fruit or ice the same as you would in any third world nation.

There are several cases of Cholera and Hepatis A listed for Cuba, I recommend that you check the CDC prior to your visit regarding precautions and routine vaccinations (Health Information for Travelers to Cuba, 2016). This is especially important if you are not staying on a cruise ship, luxury hotel or resort and are visiting small villages and/or relatives.

Using a rest room in parts of Cuba can be quite an experience. You might just have a hole in the floor and have to pay 5 CUCs for a bucket of water and a glass to pour over your hands.

It is advisable to bring your own tissue paper, handy wipes and hand disinfectant.

Always wash or sanitize your hands prior to eating. I usually recommend that you bring anti-diarrhea medication and a medication like "Colace" just in case of constipation. It is also advisable to take a Probiotic to aid in digestion especially after you have a bout of diarrhea.

Free Health Care and Pharmacies

Yes, the Cuban government provides free health care for all citizens, to a point. My guide said that it is easy to get aspirin or basic medications at government pharmacies, but it costs out of pocket for other drugs. Personally, I would not visit Cuba unless I were on a cruise ship where there is sufficient medical care and a staff of well trained professionals.

The condition of the "free clinics" for Cuban Citizens are deplorable and are not up to U.S. and European standards. I've been informed that the conditions are so bad that patients might come home with more problems than they had prior to their stay.

On page 28 there are Exclusive Photos of Havana's Hospital Clínico Quirúrgico de 26 taken in May of 2011 by Julio Muñoz, who left Cuba to come to the United States in 1990 and went back in 2011 to visit his family in Cuba. (Free Healthcare?, 2011)

During his stay in Havana, he had to take his aunt to the Emergency Room at Hospital Clínico Quirúrico to receive medical care for one of her fingers. These are the hospitals where Cubans have to go because they do not have the hard currency to pay the Castro brothers, like their foreign patients can.

0-7 We went by this Farmacia in Cienfuegos.

I've included a couple of Muñoz's pictures below more can be seen by visiting this link (Free Health Care?, 2011). Photos courtesy of TheRealCuba.com and Julio Muñoz.

Figure 0-2: "The X-Ray Room A ripped mattress; ancient equipment (probably pre-Castro era) and the ceiling caving in."

Figure 0-3: "The Lab Believe it or not, this is the Laboratory! Gracias Fidel!"

Figure 0-4: "The Emergency Room Medical supplies that had been used on other patients could be seen on the floor." (Free Health Care?, 2011)

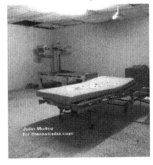

Is it Safe?

The country receives more than 2 million tourists annually and many are return visitors from Britain, and Canada. Safety is a primary concern for many travelers these days. Despite what some people may think, Cuba is a safe destination with a relatively low crime rate and almost no violent crime. Many travelers are overwhelmed by how inviting and friendly the Cuban people are toward American tourists. While the political isolation has prevented Cuba from modernizing at the same pace as most Western nations, Cuba has dramatically improved its tourism infrastructure. Hotel choices range from inexpensive government-run facilities to world-class resorts and luxury hotels. Many of the cars remain classic - a treat for automobile aficionados - but tour buses are often more modern and reliable.

From a health perspective, Cuba doesn't pose any major health concerns except for Hepatitis A for those drinking tap water in remote areas with bad sanitation. Health concerns for travelers in Cuba are significantly lower than in Mexico and many of the Caribbean nations.

Basically, Cuba is safe for travelers except for petty crooks and internet crime if you are lucky enough to get service. The country has a very low crime rate compared to other destinations around the world. The people are friendly towards the American visitor but they charge for everything including photos that you might take of the street performers, people smoking cigars, etc. And they are not shy about asking for the favorite charge of 5 CUCs or $5 Dollars U.S. to take photo(s) or "friendly advice". They can be quite aggressive even for unsolicited charactures drawn as you pass. The amazing thing is that the "tip" isn't negotiable by the citizens. All CUCs are collected by armed government agents each day. Don't be afraid to say no to them.

Best Time to Visit

Cuba is a warm, temperate climate year-round with lows of 70 degrees F and highs seldom greater than 87 degrees F. It is humid from May through October during the rainy season. In the winter, Cuba experiences peak tourism. Hurricanes most likely hit Cuba from September through October.

Peak Season is from December 22nd to March 1st

High Season is from April 1st to March 31st

Mid-Season is in April

Low Season is from May 1st to July 14th

Summer High Season is from July 15th to August 31st

Middle Season is from September 1st to December 12th

Peak Season is also during FIHAV (HAV International Trade Fair): From November 1st to the 30th

Languages

Cuban people who deal with tourists are fluent in English but the general population's main language is Spanish. The guides that accompanied my group were literate and spoke English. They were friendly and very anxious to make sure that all of our questions were addressed. Note: all guides were employed by the Cuban Government and talking points included government propaganda. My main complaint was that we could not hear them talk unless we were very close. My second concern was the way were directed to purchase gifts and Cuban Cigars at shops that we were assured provided those items at great prices. WRONG! I found similar items at government run shops for less. I suggest that you look at the prices charged in cruise ports prior to purchasing cigars, shirts or keepsakes elsewhere.

Two Official Government Currencies

Moneda Nacional (MN)

The National Currency is the one that Cuban citizens use to purchase goods and services not provided by the Cuban Government. MN have faces on the front of the bills and coins.

Cadeca Convertible peso (CUC)

Most tourists will only see and deal with the CUC, which is pegged at an artificial exchange rate of 1CUC= $0.86 USD. To avoid taking a 14% hit on every dollar you change, my advice is to bring Euros or Canadian Dollars, which have much more favorable exchange rates. For example, 1 Euro = CUC 1.27, so you are better off bringing currency other than the US Dollar. Wherever you exchange money (at the airport on arrival, at your hotel, or at exchange places called CADECA) the rates are all the same. Remember that

Americans cannot use US credit cards or travelers cheques in Cuba, so bring enough cash to cover your expenses.

> Beware: when you receive change some locals will cheat you as The CUCs and the national peso look almost identical. Do not accept any coins or bills with images of faces.

Traveler's checks are not honored, and there is no way to apply for a refund for checks lost in Cuba. As of January 2015, it is legal for travelers to Cuba to use credit cards issued by U.S. banks.

I exchanged my U.S. Dollars for Canadian Dollars in the United States before I left to avoid the extra 10% charge that the Cuban Government levies on American citizens in addition to the 13% normal charge for the balance of the world currencies. My friend Ignacio told me to "buy about $100-150 CUCs at a time, so you don't get stuck with a lot of CUCs at the end of your trip. When you buy CUCs, ask for small bills. You will be amazed how difficult it is to get change in certain places, so the smaller the denominations you carry with you, the better. Also, keep coins with you, as many bathrooms expect a CUC 0.25 'donation' as you leave."

0-1 Armed guards in Havana. Notice the burlap sack carried by the last person on the right? Photo Courtesy of Linda O.

You should bring more money than you think you need because locations visited by tourists are very overpriced. There are few bargains, I paid $40 U.S. for a button down Cuban Shirt. The prices were similar to the prices of the same shirts made and delivered from businesses in Miami that produce the same shirt.

When we ate in a Bar or Privately run Paladar we paid in CUCs. Remember that CUCs are not used by citizens in Cuba and they are turned over to government police every day. We saw some of these people come into the bar that we went to one day. Armed guards stood at the door, hands on their weapons, while the balance went up to the bar; one with a burlap bag and the other two on each side as they scanned the room with hands on their weapons. The bar tender pulled out a stack of CUCs 4 inches thick and proceeded to count out the cash and then handed it over to be placed in the bag. As fast as they walked in they walked out. I didn't take the picture that accompanies this article because I was told that if I were caught taking pictures of the police, military or customs people that I would be detained and sent to jail. But my friend from another group took the picture as they walked down the hill outside of the bar.

Cadeca Exchange Offices

U.S. Dollars can be exchanged for Convertible pesos or CUCs tourism a government run exchange offices called the Cadeca. These offices operate a limited number of hours per day at airports, cruise terminals, and at certain hotels.

Use of Credit / Debit Cards

First U.S. Bank to Issue a Credit Card - On June 8, 2014, Stonegate Bank President David Seleski announced that the small Florida is the first U.S. Bank to issue a credit card for use in Cuba. This card will make it easier for U.S. Citizens to make purchases on the island. (Florida bank issues first U.S. credit card for use in Cuba, 2016)

The Pompano Beach Florida-based Stonegate Bank started taking applications for the Master Card which can be used at government run businesses and a small number of private luxury hotels and restaurants that have the point-of-sale devices installed. Unless you have a Cuban Government approved credit card you will need to pay cash for your purchases. I found that most establishments did not and probably will not have credit card devices because of the poor internet. In rural villages you will need to have CUCs because foreign currencies, even U.S. Dollars will not be accepted. You should bring $400 in cash that can be converted into CUCs at government exchange offices. An 11.25% commission is charged for use of credit cards.

Tipping

The Cuban Government has been known to confiscate "gifts" that some Americans bring with them to give to school children. On my trip a couple purchased soccer balls, hats, pencils and crayons with the idea that they could give them to school children that they might meet. They were disappointed when they were told at the customs gate that we had to go through going into and out of each city that they needed to bring them back to the ship or hand them over to the Cuban Customs officers. (By the way those people are very serious about their jobs and were all business. So, don't talk to them as you might when going through customs in the rest of the world. I had the same experience as I entered and left China. Remember that there are two currencies in Cuba, one for the Cuban Citizens and one for tourists and the Cuban Government. Every time you give a tip of 5 CUCs ($5 U.S.) your money goes into the coffers of the Cuban Government and the Elites in Cuba. So, what should you do?

According to an anonymous Havana Student: "Realizing that good intentions are only creating a bigger gap between rich and poor in a society in which the system intends that all are equal, and that years of random gifting in Cuba has nothing for the progress of the country and made it a constant hassle for many tourists to visit? Turning doctors and scholars into resort bartenders or street pimps and university graduates into prostitutes - instead of teachers, nurses or professors.

Here are two things that can be done:

1. Tip per local standards and realize that there are other people in the 40 other rooms at the resort tipping as well. And leave any material item and larger cash sum with organizations in Cuba that have a much better overview of who needs the aid and a way to get the aid there. None of which is in any way possible to know for a regular tourist. If it is the 'save-the-world' gene that has you handing out, consider helping in countries that are in dire need of help. Look no further than Cuba's nearest neighbor, Haiti, for instance. A starving Haitian living in the streets of Port Au Prince would probably be shocked to see well-fed Cubans being handed gifts and money just because they hold that one quality that in the mindset of many tourists qualifies them for immediate material aid: They are Cuban.

2. Accept that Cuba is Cuba and not Canada, UK or Italy. That the world is a varied place, and that there are other ways to live and make a country go around than what most tourists are used to. And go there with a solid conscience that the simple fact that you are traveling there makes a huge impact on Cuba's economy. A contribution that is already being spread out into every corner of the country through all the above-mentioned government initiatives (Food, housing, school, hospitals). And thus, head there knowing that the trip-purchase itself is doing Cubans good.

The greatest gift is respect and friendship. That is what 'real' Cubans are interested in. The Cubans who beg for the shirt off your back or the soap in your bathroom or the peso in your pocket, may not need those items at all. And by giving randomly a tourist is only making sure that begging and hassling tourists stays a profitable business. And that more Cubans are turning to this way of life. In effect that does nothing good for Cuba - and nothing good for any tourist visiting Cuba. (Gifts - Cuba Forum, 2017)

Gifts and U.S. Customs

Keep in mind that there is a per diem amount of money that the U.S. Treasury Department allows visitors to spend. The most recently published maximum for Havana was $166 per day and $125 in all other localities. (Travants, 2015)

Shopping

Cuba sells imported electronics and other goods, mainly to Cubans whose relatives send money from overseas or who earn dollars or convertible pesos either legitimately in tourism or on the black market.

The hard-currency shops sell everything you'd expect in a small-scale supermarket: food, shampoo, liquor, clothes, hardware, electronics, crafts, toys and medicine, among other things. You can find souvenirs in the hard-currency shops at tourist hotels and in the airport, as well as in Old Havana and major tourist destinations throughout Cuba.

Whatever you're buying, be aware that bargaining is common in Cuban markets. General shopping hours are Monday-Saturday 8:30 am-5:30 pm and Sunday 9 am-noon.

How can you tell if the Cuban cigars that you are buying are counterfeit?

First, the Cuban cigar ash is a distinctive dark gray while non-Cuban cigars burn with a white ash.

Second, the final wrapper of authentic Cuban cigars have 3 individual wrappers that you can easily see.

Third, handmade Cuban cigars are not wrapped in cellophane except for the 3/5 pak Petacas.

Cuban cigars are popular souvenirs, so tourists can expect to be approached on the street by people selling what appear to be top brands (such as Cohiba or Montecristo's) at rock-bottom prices. I found the prices for cigars higher in shops recommended by "tour guides" and people in the city; I believe that they get paid for recommending business for the high cost cigars. The least expensive authentic Cuban cigars were available in the government sanctioned stores in the cruise terminals. The same is true when purchasing artwork, sculptures, or paintings. Beware, there is a 25% tax on all artwork charged by Cuban Customs Enforcement prior to leaving Cuba

0-2 Havana Club Rum served in Havana

(People in our group were not aware of the charge and if they didn't have the CUCs to cover the tax the items were confiscated by the Cuban Government.)

The Cuban government allows the export of only 23 undocumented cigars, and any cigar box without a hologram seal and a proper receipt from a licensed store will be confiscated at Cuban customs (all baggage is scanned on departure). I saw boxes of 25 aluminum-encased Romeo y Julietas for roughly CUC100 or $100 U.S. While a box of Cohiba Esplendidos cost approximately CUC250 or $250 U.S., more or less. The best deal in Cuba is on a handmade humidor—all sizes are available. They are first-rate and make great gifts or mementos. Since October of 2016, U.S. visitors are legally permitted to bring back up to $400 U.S. worth of goods, including tobacco and alcohol.

Rum is another big seller with visitors. I recommend the Havana Club and Ron Caney brands. If you can afford it, select the Matusalem Anejo, a delicious smoky rum that has ripened for at least 15 years in old oak casks. Also recommended is the Havana Club Gran Reserva. Other varieties are a lot cheaper. A Paticruzado or a Guayabita de Pinar may only cost CUC5, but their thin glass bottles break easily. Although street vendors might offer bottles for less they may be watered down. Bottles purchased in Cuba that don't have the tax stamp may also be confiscated when you leave Cuba. For a great selection, try La Casa del Tabaco y Ron in Havana Vieja or the Fundacion Distileria Havana Club next to the Rum Museum in Havana. Or just get your bottle at the well-stocked airport shop in Havana on the way home.

The best craft market takes place at Centro Cultural Almacen San Jose, on Avenida del Puerto in Old Havana. There, you'll find Cuban painters, sketchers and sculptors selling their work, as well as other vendors offering handmade clothing, dishes and trinkets, including lacework and hand-embroidered clothing.

Look for old books and stamps (including stamps of the former Soviet Union) at the open-air market in Plaza de Armas; note that it is illegal to take old stamps out of the country. You can also find original Cuban paintings or prints, CDs and tapes of Cuban music, and Che Guevara T-shirts (Artex stores and Casa de la Musica are good places to look).

Best Guayabera would be ordering one from a private tailor. But as I guess you will not be able to wait the time they need to get it ready, you could have two choices:

1. Shop "El Quitrin" in Obispo bet Mercaderes and Sag Ignacio, Old Havana. This is a shop where they have best selection made in Cuba because the workshop is next to the store. You can order a tailor made Guayaberra in this shop.
2. Shop "La Casa de La Guayabera" in O'Reilly & Tacon Streets, Old Havana.

Outside Havana, the best shopping is in Trinidad, where dozens of artisans sell their wares at street stalls. Particularly impressive are the lacework tablecloths and women's wear, as well as clever re-creations of 1950s

American autos made from tin cans or papier-Mache.

U.S. citizens returning from Cuba are subject to stiff government restrictions on the import of Cuban products:

There is a huge distinction between peso and hard-currency shops (which accept only CUCs or euros). The former, aimed solely at Cubans, are virtually empty and stock inferior Cuban-made items; the latter have proliferated and sell imported electronics and other goods, mainly to Cubans whose relatives send money from overseas or who

Beware, there is a 25% tax on all artwork charged by Cuban Customs Enforcement prior to leaving Cuba (People in our group were not aware of the charge and if they didn't have the CUCs to cover the tax the items were confiscated by the Cuban Government.) You may also need a special license to take quality art out of the country, as precious artworks and antiques are considered part of the national patrimony.

See & Do:

Internet and Communications

Internet

The better hotels in Havana usually have an internet center, where you buy minutes by the quarter hour. When using the internet, access will be restricted to certain news-oriented sites, but you will be able to pull up your email at Gmail, Yahoo, etc. The problem with the internet in Cuba is that it is government run and you can expect Wi-Fi at dial up speeds. My belief is that I wouldn't count on using the internet because it is spotty at best and very expensive. The only Cuban citizens who can use the internet are college students selected by the government.

Newspapers

There are no newspapers for sale in Cuba other than Granma, the official newspaper of the Cuban government. Many hotels do have access to BBC or CNN, so you have some idea of what's going on in the world.

Phone and Cellular Service

Before I left for my trip to Cuba I checked a couple of carriers to see if I could use my global phone in Cuba. I was assured that I could but I discovered that my Verizon phone did not work in Cuba although I was told that it and phones from Sprint could be used.

The next best thing to do if you have an unlocked GSM-capable mobile phone would be to rent a SIM card from Cubacel (ETECSA's mobile phone arm). Using this SIM Card will allow you to use your mobile phone in Cuba. Cubatel's SIM cards have pre-paid minutes equaling 40, 20, or 10 (CUC$) Cuban convertible pesos (US $40, $20, or $10) There is also a CUC $3 (US$3) rental fee each day for the SIM card. When renting a mobile phone or a SIM card the texting and per-minute call charges fees (as listed below). Note: All of this is subject to change. (Telecommunications FAQs for Travelers to Cuba, 2016)

0-3 Phone in Cuba (photo courtesy of Linda Oster-Safier)

All other individuals wishing to use the phone from any public phone both found throughout the country would have to purchase a "Tarjeta Propia" phone card at ETECSA to make phone calls in Cuba or rent a basic phone to use there. One of my guides said that it took him one full year to save enough money to buy the cellular phone that he was using on the job. And he can only use email and the phone, no internet.

To call the United States using a pre-paid calling card, follow these steps (Telecommunications FAQs for Travelers to Cuba, 2016):

- Dial 166, then dial the card code, followed by the hash key (#).
- Dial 119 (the international line access code), then 1 (the U.S. country code).
- Enter the ten-digit area code and phone number you wish to call, followed by the hash key.

Mobile Phone Service in Cuba: American cellular networks (i.e. Verizon, AT&T) do not work in Cuba. When traveling to Cuba, you can either purchase a SIM card[1] that will allow an unlocked smartphone to work in Cuba or rent a basic mobile phone to use in Cuba.

---

[1] Cuba holds a tight rein on telecommunications. For as little as $39.95 SIM Cards may be available for purchase: http://www.onesimcard.com/?64421 They cover 162 countries; include free incoming calls and text messages worldwide; outgoing calls as low as $0.25/min, mobile data (3G/2G Data) in 130+ countries from $0.03/MB.

Can people in the United States call me in Cuba?

> *Remember Google's announcement in 2015? The company said that it would install Free Wi-Fi antennas and wire the whole country.* Jose Ramon Machado Ventura, 85, Secretary of the Cuban Communist Party responded with a Big NO. In the state run newspaper, Juventud Rebelde, he said: "Everyone knows why there isn't more Internet access in Cuba, because it is costly. There are some who want to give it to us for free, but they don't do it so that the Cuban people can communicate... Instead their objective is to penetrate us and do ideological work to achieve a new conquest. We must have Internet, but in our way, knowing that the imperialists intend to use it to destroy the Revolution."

Yes, people in the United States can call you in Cuba if you are using an operating phone in Cuba.

Prices for calls to Cuba from the United States vary and depend on the provider and the caller's plan. You should check with your provider about the cost of making a call to Cuba using its service prior to making the call, as calling without an international calling plan or similar arrangement can cost several dollars per minute. To call from the United States, the caller will need to dial 011 (or + sign from a mobile phone), followed by 53 (Cuba's country code), followed by the Cuban phone number, which consists of six to eight digits for landlines (including the area code) or eight digits for mobile phones.

Example (calling Cuba from a U.S. landline): 011-53-5555-5555

Example (calling Cuba from a U.S. mobile phone): +53-5555-5555

Can I access the Internet in Cuba?

On my visit I discovered that Wi-Fi and internet coverage is spotty at best. You will see Cubans in parks and at hotel bars that have authority to use the internet. Currently only government people and academics have been given the right to use the internet by the government. If you are fortunate enough to get internet, don't expect the high-speed internet that we've become accustom to in the United States. Remember the dial up days?

I expect that within the next few years that the Cuban government's communication arm will provide more ability for visitors to use their phones and the internet. Currently you are more likely to find government run "telepuntos" (small internet cafes) in the larger cities like Havana and Santiago de Cuba. If you are staying at a larger hotel, then you might be able to use their business and computer center access to the internet and phone service which comes at a premium.

There are extensive lists of locations that offer Wi-Fi throughout Cuba but I've decided not to list them because they change all the time and are unreliable. I'm told that international airports (Havana, Cienfuegos, Camaguey, Holguin, Santiago, Varadero) do offer Wi-Fi service. (FCC: FAQs for Travelers to Cuba, 2016)

Transportation and Maps

Cuban Citizen Transportation

Use offline maps or preload your Google Maps. The Cuban Government is in control of all transportation on the Island. The Very few citizens have

vehicles and used shared transportation. Depending upon the license plate the transportation is sharable or not sharable. It was interesting to note the license plates on the cars. All Plates starting with the letters P (private), B (government) have to pick up citizens, not tourists, that are walking along the road. T (tourist transportation), F & M (military and/or police), E (embassy), plates are exempt from this requirement. The speed limits in cities is 35 miles per hour and the speed limit on the highway is 65 miles per hour. People with a private plate have been known to be fined if they are transporting foreigners without a license to do so. My friend in the travel business documented the various types when she visited Cuba on her trip from Mexico.

Travel by Bus

You will be able to visit all major cities and travel all around the country by bus if you can find one and if there's room. Viazul is the one that takes tourists traveling independently. The problem with the transportation system in Cuba is that it is not reliable at this time. You should go to the bus terminal at least one hour before scheduled departure. Havana buses cost CUC 5 cents.

Vintage Taxi Cuba

If you wish to take a shared taxi, or Almendrone, negotiate the price before you get in the vehicle. Drivers will always try to get more after the ride is complete so hold your ground. And foreigners always have to pay more than locals. The drivers usually park in front bus stations and bus stops to pick up people unable to get on the bus.

Vintage car taxis have a set route usually along the *Malecón*. If you want to take a ride in a 1940s/1950s American Chevrolet, Oldsmobile, or Pontiac, it will cost about CUC10 per ride. They are for tourists to ride along a select route in Havana. I met fellow tourists that were able to rent a vintage car and driver for a trip to see Ernest

0-4 Vintage car at Finca Vigia (Hemingway's Home)

Hemingway's compound at Finca Vigia. So, it is possible to find someone who will drive you around for a day. As always, negotiate the price prior to getting into the car.

Depending upon the license plate the transportation is sharable or not sharable. It was interesting to note the license plates on the cars. All Plates starting with the letters P (private), B (government) have to pick up citizens, not tourists, that are walking along the road. T (tourist transportation), F & M (military and/or police), E (embassy), plates are exempt from this requirement.

Transportation in Cuba

(Photographs courtesy of Eva Holguin)

Although most citizens do not own an automobile they manage to get

around the island using public and shared rides. In the country side you will see more people hopping on a vehicle that passes or they may own a bicycle or horse that they use for transportation. The law states that if you own a private or sharable vehicle you must stop and pick up people who are hitch-

hiking along your route of travel.

In this group of photographs, you see several modes of transportation with passengers who jumped on as the vehicle passed. Depending upon where

you travel within the bounds of the island the mode of transportation changes. The yellow pods above can be rented in some cities. They accommodate two to three people. Many tourists find this an interesting way to tour the city if they don't want to hire a vintage car taxi.

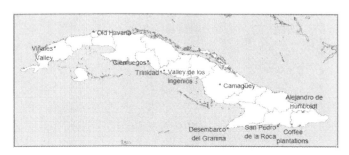

List of World Heritage Sites in Cuba

As a Level 2 Member of The United Nations Educational, Scientific and Cultural Organization (UNESCO) World Heritage Sites I am always interested in the major destinations that the organization lists in each country that I visit. In Cuba they list several that I enumerate in the list below. Location of sites can be seen in the map above.

Old Havana

Even thou Christopher Columbus landed on the south side of Cuba in 1492, it wasn't until 1519 that Spanish settled on the north-western bay, now known as Havana. By the 17th century, because of its proximity to Florida and the Caribbean it became a very valuable ship building center. In Old Havana, you can find buildings following Baroque and Neoclassical architecture. The Cathedral of Havana, La Cabaña and the Great Theatre of Havana are examples of the historic building that many tourists visit while visiting Havana, Cuba. (UNESCO: Old Havana and its Fortifications, 2016)

Trinidad

In the early part of the 16th century the city of Trinidad was settled. The Spanish Explorer, Cortés left the port of Trinidad to conquer Mexico in 1518. Because of the huge success of the sugar business the city prospered and is still an important producer of sugar cane today. In addition to the presence of sugar mills, you will find tobacco plantations and cattle ranches. (UNESCO: Trinidad and the Valley de los Ingenios, 2016), (UNESCO: Trinidad, Cuba, 2016)

San Pedro de la Roca Castle, Santiago de Cuba

The large fort was built to defend the important port of Santiago de Cuba. The design of the fortification was based on Italian and Renaissance architecture. The complex of magazines, bastions, and batteries is one of the most complete and well-preserved Spanish-American defense fortifications. (UNESCO: San Pedro de la Roca Castle, Santiago de Cuba, 2016)

Desembarco del Granma National Park - Granma

The national park is named for the yacht which carried Fidel Castro, Raúl Castro, Che Guevara and the other 79 members of the 26th of July Movement to Cuba to overthrow Fulgencio Batista. The park features a unique karst topography with features such as cliffs, terraces, and waterfalls. (UNESCO: Desembarco del Granma National Park, n.d.)

Viñales Valley - Pinar del Río Province

The village of Viñales was founded in 1875 after the expansion of tobacco cultivation in the surrounding valley. The Valley features a karst topography, vernacular architecture, and traditional cultivation methods. The Valley was also the site of various military engagements in the Cuban War of

Independence and Cuban Revolution. (UNESCO: Viñales Valley, 2016), (UNESCO: Viñales (Cuba), 2016)

Santiago de Cuba and Guantánamo

During the 19th and early 20th centuries, eastern Cuba was primarily involved with coffee cultivation. The remnants of the plantations display the techniques used in the difficult terrain, as well as the economic and social significance of the plantation system in Cuba and the Caribbean. (UNESCO: Archaeological Landscape of the First Coffee Plantations in the South-East of Cuba, 2016)

Alejandro de Humboldt National Park - Holguín and Guantánamo

The rivers that originate in the high elevations are among the largest of the Insular Caribbean. The park exhibits a wide array of geology types. (UNESCO: Alejandro de Humboldt National Park, 2016)

Urban Historic Centre of Cienfuegos - Cienfuegos

Cienfuegos was founded in 1819 as a Spanish colony, though its first inhabitants were French immigrants. It became a trade center in coffee, sugar cane, and tobacco because of its location on the Bay of Cienfuegos. Because of its establishment in the later colonial period, the architecture has more modern influences: including modern urban planning. (UNESCO: Urban Historic Centre of Cienfuegos, 2016)

Historic Centre of Camagüey - Camagüey

Camagüey is among the first seven villages founded by the Spanish in Cuba, first settled in 1528. The irregular organization of the city is distinct from the typical, orderly construction of most other Spanish settlements. This maze-like style was influenced by medieval European ideas and traditional construction methods of early immigrant masons and construction workers. (UNESCO: Historic Centre of Camagüey, 2016)

Accommodations

This part of any industry fluctuates on a regular business throughout the world. American citizens cannot legally book any travel to Cuba except through authorized travel providers. Because of the changing policies and economic climate in Cuba I will not be covering it in this book. Please consult with a certified travel professional before you decide to Cuba.

Hotels

All hotels in Cuba are government owned and some are managed by the major hotel chains. In many cases the chain built the hotel and then the government took it over and allows the chain to manage it.

Cuban B&Bs - "Casa Particular"

There are several "Casa Particulars" in the major cities. Privately run by a Cuban family and monitored by the Cuban Government. I have been told that you can find reasonable Air B and B's in Havana.

Resorts

The Canadians, Europeans have been visiting Cuban Resorts since the early 1990's. The resorts are government owned and managed by international groups. They are located on some of the most beautiful beaches in the Caribbean. Some approved American based tour groups do book some of their itineraries at these resorts for use in the evening. Due to the regulations covering travel to Cuba the resorts should not be considered the final destination but one accommodation provided during a "People to People" educational tour.

Restaurants

Government

The Cuban government operates many of the largest restaurants found in and around destinations visited by tourists. The quality of the food tends to be higher than with private restaurants, with some exceptions. During my visit, many of my group were journalists working on a story. Not once during our visit did we visit a Paladar. Friends of mine in other groups did eat at Paladars and had mixed reactions. The citizen owned restaurants were friendlier beyond providing service. I came to the conclusion that most dignitaries, educational institutions and journalists will not be directed to Paladars.

Private – "Paladars", Citizen owned restaurants

Don't eat from the really cheap local restaurants, many of us are used to eating street food, from very cheap places, but Cuba was an exception. It is common to see places selling pizza and ice cream or other meals for a fraction of what they should cost and charged in CUP (like 10 CUP or $0.50 and much less). These foods, while cheap, are considered "garbage" by locals since they are done with local products of the lowest quality possible.

Not surprisingly, markets there don't offer much variety since they focus on selling items of first need to locals – which don't include sweets and snacks. You may find a few snacks here and there, but those are rare, and there will not be a lot of varieties.

Havana
Havana district map

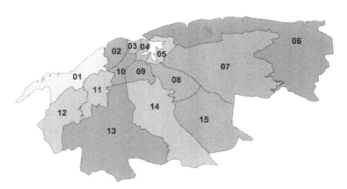

Districts

The city is divided into 15 municipalities – or boroughs, which are further subdivided into 105 wards (consejos populares). (Numbers refer to map).

Playa: Santa Fe, Siboney, Cubanacán, Ampliación Almendares, Miramar, Sierra, Ceiba, Buena Vista.

1. Plaza de la Revolución: El Carmelo, Vedado-Malecón, Rampa, Príncipe, Plaza, Nuevo Vedado-Puentes Grandes, Colón-Nuevo Vedado, Vedado.
2. Centro Habana: Cayo Hueso, Pueblo Nuevo, Los Sitios, Dragones, Colón.
3. La Habana Vieja : Prado, Catedral, Plaza Vieja, Belén, San Isidro, Jesús María, Tallapiedra.
4. Regla : Guaicanimar, Loma Modelo, Casablanca.
5. La Habana del Este : Camilo Cienfuegos, Cojímar, Guiteras, Alturas de Alamar, Alamar Este, Guanabo, Campo Florido, Alamar-Playa.
6. Guanabacoa : Mañana-Habana Nueva, Villa I, Villa II, Chivas-Roble, Debeche-Nalon, Hata-Naranjo, Peñalver-Bacuranao, Minas-Barreras.
7. San Miguel del Padrón: Rocafort, Luyanó Moderno, Diezmero, San Francisco de Paula, Dolores-Veracruz, Jacomino.
8. Diez de Octubre : Luyanó, Jesús del Monte, Lawton, Vista Alegre, Acosta, Sevillano, La Víbora, Santos Suárez, Tamarindo.

9. Cerro: Latinoamericano, Pilar-Atares, Cerro, Las Cañas, El Canal, Palatino, Armada.
10. Marianao : CAI-Los Ángeles, Pocito-Palmas, Zamora-Cocosolo, Libertad, Pogoloti-Belén-Finlay, Santa Felicia.
11. La Lisa : Alturas de La Lisa, Balcón Arimao, El Cano-Valle Grande-Bello 26 y Morado, Punta Brava, Arroyo Arenas, San Agustín, Versalles-Coronela.
12. Boyeros: Santiago de Las Vegas, Nuevo Santiago, Boyeros, Wajay, Calabazar, Altahabana-Capdevila, Armada-Aldabo.
13. Arroyo Naranjo: Los Pinos, Poey, Víbora Park, Mantilla, Párraga, Calvario-Fraternidad, Guinera, Eléctrico, Managua, Callejas.
14. Cotorro: San Pedro-Centro Cotorro, Santa Maria del Rosario, Lotería, Cuatro Caminos, Magdalena-Torriente, Alberro."

Notes on Cuba: Havana sightseeing [Source 01/29/2013 Posted by Ignacio Maza]

Havana

Havana, Cuba's capital, has a population of about 2.5 million. Overall, the city is in a state of decay and disrepair, aside from a few renovated buildings and major tourist areas like parts of Old Havana (La Habana Vieja). The city is very spread out and you will need at least 3 days to see the major sights. Here are some ideas as to how best to organize your time, and places that are well worth visiting.

Havana attracts over a million tourists annually, the Official Census for Havana reports that in 2010 the city was visited by 1,176,627 international tourists, a +20.0% increase from 2005.

The city has long been a popular attraction for tourists. Between 1915 and 1930, Havana hosted more tourists than any other location in the Caribbean. The influx was due in large part to Cuba's proximity to the United States, where restrictive prohibition on alcohol and other pastimes stood in stark contrast to the island's traditionally relaxed attitude to leisure pursuits. A pamphlet published by E.C. Kropp Co., Milwaukee, WI, between 1921 and 1939 promoting tourism in Havana, Cuba, can be found in the University of Houston Digital Library, Havana, Cuba.

Landmarks and historical centers

Habana Vieja / Plaza Vieja: (or main square) in central Havana in 1762 during the British occupation. This plaza in Old Havana was also the site of executions, processions, bullfights, and fiestas.

Fortress San Carlos de la Cabaña, is a fortress located on the east side of the Havana bay, La Cabaña is the most impressive fortress from colonial times, specifically its walls constructed at the end of the 18th century. Every evening there is a cannon ceremony at the fortress that has taken place for over 400 years. Due to pirate attacks by the massive walls were built to protect Havana. Inhabitants had to gain

entry before 9 PM each evening prior to the firing of the cannon. The ceremony is depicted in the photo (Photo courtesy of Linda Safier, 2016) is now known as "El Canonazo"

El Capitolio Nacional: built in 1929 as the Senate and House of Representatives, the Capitolio is smaller than the U.S. Capital building in Washington, D.C. You can see the dome from just about anywhere in the city. In the rotunda the 3rd largest statue in the world stands, "La Estatua de la República". Today, the Museo Nacional de Historia Natural (the National Museum of Natural History) and the Cuban Academy of Sciences reside within the building. The Museum of Natural History hosts the largest natural history collection in Cuba. (Havana, 2017)

Behind the Capitol is a fenced in park where the soil from every country in Latin America is deposited. It is symbolic of Cuba's ties to its neighbors.

El Morro Castle

At the east side of the entrance to Havana bay stands the Castle of Tres Reyes del Morro (AKA El Morro Castle and lighthouse), a fortress guarding the bay; After the threat from pirates entering the harbor grew Morro Castle was built. The picture below is the castle as we entered the bay on our ship.

Built in the 16th century on the western side of Havan harbor lies the small fortress of Castillo San Salvador de la Punta. Fortress was vital in the defense of Havana during the early centuries of colonization. It houses some twenty old guns and military antiques. (Havana Cuba the Lost Island, 2011)

Christ of Havana: In 1958 the marble statue of Christ was erected to bless the city. It stands on the eastern side of the bay atop a hillside. The 66-foot statue was under repair when I visited.

The Great Theatre of Havana: is an opera house and concert hall that is the home of the National Ballet of Cuba and occasional hosts performances by the National Opera. The García Lorca Theater is the largest in Cuba.

(Photo courtesy of Cuba Tourism, 2016)

The Malecón / Sea wall:

The Malecón is the avenue that runs for 5 miles along the northern side of the city and the seawall separates the roadway from the Atlantic Ocean. The Malecón (AKA Avenida de Maceo) is the most popular avenue of Havana, it is known for its sunsets, during the day I saw people sunbathing and fishing from the wall. We were told that it is a great meeting place for young couples and old alike because it is free. (Photo courtesy of Fathom Cruise Line, 2016)

We saw lots of old cars driving along this boulevard. Here are some of the photos that I shot of the old cars on northern sea side boulevard.

More Old Cars on the Malecón!

Take a ride in a vintage 57 Chevy, Oldsmobile or Pontiac for about 10 CUCs per ride (approximately 10 U.S. dollars), be sure to set the price prior to taking your ride. 1940s/1950s American car (usually Chevrolets, Oldsmobile's, Pontiacs) for about CUC10 per ride. That's approximately 10 U.S. Dollars, be sure to negotiate the rate "prior" to getting in the car.

Yea, I know I went crazy…

Vedado

Hotel Nacional de Cuba

The hotel and casino first opened in the 1930's and became famous in the 1950s. It has hosted presidents, Winston Churchill, Al Capone, movie stars, and celebrities traveling through Havana over the last 80 years. The hotel is on a hill on the south side of the Malecón located in the neighborhood known as Vedado. To enter the hotel, you drive up the palm-studded avenue and walk into a grand, noisy, lobby with high ceilings and lots of history. The hotel has 2 pools, vast gardens and

The National hosts "Cabaret Parisien" an evening that showcases the "soul" of Cuba. The program tells the story of Cuba in a traditional cabaret fashion. During the cabaret you see how the history of Cuba was influenced by the Indo American, Spanish and African cultures.

This function is featured in the itineraries of People-to-People programs like the one for passengers on Fathom Adonia Ship. It is suggested that you dress "smart casual" and be over 17 years of age.

terraces, and overlooks the Malecon and the El Morro fortress in the distance. The hotel rooms, elevators, beds, and hallways all need to be renovated. Service is also poor due to the huge volume of people just visiting. I would recommend going there for a drink after dinner but stay on a ship or in another hotel!

During the Cuban Missile crisis in the first part of the 1960's the hotel served as military headquarters for Fidel Castro and Che Guevara. A museum is open to present Cuba's side to the conflict is in the hotel. The Art Deco architecture is prevalent in these old buildings that are in Old Havana. My friend Ignacio does not recommend staying there because of the poor condition of the building but it is worth spending the evening visiting the bar in the hotel. From the bar you can see the roadway and the Atlantic Ocean to the north. The photo was taken from the top of the hotel across the street, the La Torra Restaurant, where we ate lunch.

"Plaza de la Revolución"

The "Plaza de la Revolución" with the nearby Museo de la Revolución &

0-1 Statue of Marti in front of the memorial.

is 31st largest city square in the world is known as "Revolution Square", measuring 72,000 square meters. The museum is located behind the photo above in the former Presidential Palace, with the yacht Granma on display behind the museum. In the photo above, you see The José Martí Memorial, which features Havana's highest landmark, 350 ft. tall tower with a 59' statue. Open Monday to Saturday, you can see great views of the city of Havana.

Marti is the revolutionary who helped free Cuba from Spain along with the American President, Teddy Roosevelt in the last century. The Cubans refer to this war as the Cuban, Spanish and American War. (In contrast to our referral of the conflict as the Spanish American War.)

The square is important because this is where the Cuban people lined up to see Fidel Castro speak and to view his remains after his death. During his live he and others addressed millions of Cubans on Cuban holidays, notably May 1st and July. During papal visits to Cuba two Popes served Mass in the square. The first visit by Pope John Paul II was in 1998. Again in 2015, Pope Francis served Mass.

After the death of Fidel Castro in 2016, mourners lined up in this square to view his corpse at the José Martí Memorial. There were three days of mourning prior to the private internment ceremony for his family and party members.

The National Library, many government ministries, and other buildings are in and around the Plaza. Located behind the memorial is the Palace of the Revolution, the seat of the Cuban government and Communist Party. Across form the memorial are several cultural institutions as well as the offices of the Ministries of the Communications and Interior, with the faces of Che Guevara, and a quote "Hasta la Victoria Siempre" (Until the Everlasting Victory, Always) and Camilo Cienfuegos (sometimes mistaken for Fidel

Castro), with the quote "Vas bien, Fidel" (You're doing fine, Fidel). Prior to the death of Fidel Castro, both were important deceased heroes of the Cuban Revolution: (Plaza de la Revolución, 2017)

An elevator allows access the top of the José Martí Memorial.

On January 3, 2017, Cuban troops marked the 60th Anniversary of the start of the war for independence. The parade was postponed one month due to the death of Fidel Castro. The street through Revolution Square was lined with a single line of citizens viewing the Cuban troops commemorating the landing of the Castro brothers, Che and their band of revolutionaries. As Raul Castro and his family waved from the steps of the monument to Jose Marti, people like the 50-year-old engineer from Havana, Antonio Sosa, chose not to attend. Sosa says: "Everything is very uncertain at the moment, so there's more propaganda. You don't see news on news broadcast any more, just speeches Fidel gave 30 years ago." I believe that this sentiment was because the tourism boom didn't solve the cash flow problems due to the reduced oil shipments from Venezuela providing less cash for professionals and the elites in Cuba (Frank, 2017).

Necrópolis Cristóbal Colón: The Colon Cemetery is a 140-acre cemetery and open-air museum, it is one of the most famous cemeteries in Latin America and is found in Vedrado neighborhood of Havana. It's known for its beauty and magnificence and is visited by people from all over the world. The cemetery was built in 1876 on top of the Espada Cemetery and has nearly one million tombs. The cemetery is named after Christopher Columbus is noted for its many elaborately sculpted memorials. It is estimated that today the cemetery has more than 500 major mausoleums, chapels, and family vaults. Some gravestones are decorated with sculptures by Ramos Blancos, among others. (Discover Cuba, 2017) (Colon Cemetary, 2017)

The visage on page 57 is part of one of the tomb stones in the cemetery (above). On the right you see one of the most visited graves in the cemetery. The statue is of the woman who was holding a child in her hands that had to be pried from her grip. The child lived and the mother was put to rest in the grave marked by her last act while she lived.

Below is one of the most photographed buildings in Havana, it is the Chapel of Colon.

The tombs in the cemetery date back several hundred years. And are maintained by women and men who clean the stones and trim the grass out between the cracks in the cement.

The Cuban Government pays for the funerals of its citizens in cemeteries like the Cementerio de Cristóbal Colón but the cost of elaborate graves and tombs are paid for by the families of the deceased. The vehicle in the photograph on page 60 is a government car designated by the "T" for Transportation Ministry. And the family is there to bury their loved one. People are still being buried there.

Workshop at artist José Fuster's studio

Neighborhood art has been encouraged by artist José Fuster's neighborhood. Art like this is encouraged by the government and the people take pride in the upgrades to their neighborhoods. We were welcomed to the community by the son of José Fuster who is carrying on the traditions of his father. His photograph is on page 61.

Old Havana

Havana was founded almost 500 years ago, so it makes sense to start in the oldest district where the city began. There are many

options for hotel accommodations in this part of the city. The upside is that you walk out the front door and have many of the city's landmarks nearby. The downside is the noise, especially at night, and the wandering musicians and revelers coming out of bars and clubs that stay open late. Hotel Ambos Mundos (Calle Obispo 153) is where Ernest Hemingway wrote 'For whom the bell tolls' years ago in room 511, which is kept exactly as he left it.

Plaza San Francisco, is a beautiful square flanked by the church of San

Francisco. From here, continue to the Plaza Vieja, a very different 16th century square flanked mostly by residential buildings. You can get lost in Old Havana's many narrow streets, each with its own history. If you are a fan of Ernest Hemingway, you can visit La Bodeguita del Medio, where Hemingway and many other celebrities used to while away the hours. The most interesting streets in Old Havana are Obrapia and Obispo running East-West, and Calle Oficios, running North-South.

While in Old Havana, my group passed the Museo del Chocolate who's aroma permeated the streets. There you can drink their homemade hot chocolate or buy some of their famous chocolate candies. The store is located at calle Mercaderes on the corner of Amargura st. (Havana Cuba Tours, 2017) Most visitors to Cuba visit old Havana, so expect to see troops of Americans, Canadians, and Europeans walking up and down the streets, as well as Cuban musicians playing live music on many corners.

While in Old Havana, stop at the Hotel Ambos Mundos (Obispo street #153, corner of Mercaderes st), take the elevator to the roof, and have a drink and or lunch in the rooftop bar that has super views of Old Havana.

Plaza de la Catedral

Start at the Plaza de la Catedral, where the city's beautiful baroque cathedral stands and is open 10:30 AM to 3:00 PM daily, with no admission fee.

The exterior is one of the finest examples of Cuban Baroque Architecture, and is in contrast to the interior, which is fairly simple. The square is surrounded by great colonial buildings such as the Casa del Marques de Arcos and the Casa de Lombillo. There is a museum of colonial art in the house of the Conde de Bayona, also facing the square.

From here, it's a 5-minute walk to the Plaza de Armas, one of Havana's most beautiful squares.

Plaza de Armas is a "Parade Ground"

The Plaza de Armas (AKA Paseo del Prado) is a great promenade flanked by Royal Palms (the official tree of Cuba), Ceiba trees and benches, running from the sea down towards the Parque Central/Capitol area. The most beautiful buildings in this area are the former Centro Gallego, now the Gran Teatro de La Habana, an enormous, block-size building with Beaux-arts architecture, and the Capitol.

The Plaza is the spot where Havana was first founded, and the square witnessed many of Cuba's most important events. Since 1519 this area has

been used as a gathering place. In 1741 the former church's cobblestone square was renamed Plaza de Armas, the administrative center of the city, surrounded by buildings up to four hundred years old. In the center of the square is a white marble statue of Carlos Manuel de Céspedes, Father of the Homeland, an important figure in Cuba's wars of independence.

As we walked into the plaza we walked on a street on the west side of the plaza that is made of wood. The ironwood planks were laid down on the street to muffle the sound of horse's hoofs at night so that the governor's wife could sleep. In recent times the planks on the street have been replaced with less durable wood and are deteriorating.

South of the plaza are vendors selling newspapers and art work.

0-2 vendors selling newspapers and art work.

The fortress above is the Castillo de la Real Fuerza, Havana's first major fort and now a naval museum that traces the history of ships and shipbuilding through the ages. My friend Ignacio says, do not miss the views from the top staircase, to get a better sense of the fort (surrounded by a moat) and part of the old city.

Facing the square is Havana's most beautiful colonial building, the Palacio de los Capitanes Generales, a masterpiece of 18th century architecture, which today houses the museum of Havana's history. If you pick one museum to go to in old Havana, make this your choice. The building is open Tuesday to Sunday, and is well worth a visit. Regardless of your political views, the Museum of the Revolution is worth seeing, if only for the fact it is housed in the former Presidential Palace. If you visit, pay the extra 2CUC to visit the former offices and meeting rooms of Cuba's presidents, which are time capsules. Don't miss the secret doorway used by Batista to escape revolutionaries who were trying to kill him in a palace coup in the late 50s. This building housed the governors of Cuba during the colonial years, and was the site of Cuba's first president's swearing in ceremony in 1902.

> Tip: Pay the 1CUC at the reception desk, and visit the building's rooftop for a breathtaking view of the city.

(Ignacio Maza, 2015)

0-3 Palacio de los Capitanes Generales

0-4 Hotel Santa Isabella

Just south of the Plaza de Armas is the Hotel Santa Isabella, a 27 room five-star establishment that's centrally located in Old Havana. The cozy courtyard allowed us to get out of the heat for a little while. The hotel hosted movie stars and presidents in the past.

If you are interested in architecture, visit the Bacardi Building (headquarters of the rum distiller) at the corner of San Juan de Dios and Villegas streets, near the Parque Central. This building is a masterpiece of Cuban Art Deco, and well worth seeing.

Centro Habana

The neighborhood next to old Havana, Centro Habana is also worth visiting. The architecture is from the late 19th/early 20th century built when the walls surrounding Havana were torn down to allow for expansion.

The Eastern Bay

Across the bay from Old Havana are two famous historic fortresses, the El Morro and La Cabana which you should make time to see. Take a taxi to see them and negotiate to pay the driver to wait for you during your visit otherwise its next to impossible to get back to the city on the other side of the bay. The oldest fortress, the El Morro, was built in the 16th century to combat pirates and foreign armies trying to seize Havana. The lighthouse of El Morro is the symbol of the city has the best views of Havana, especially at sunset. The grounds around the fortresses are large offering walking paths for the adventurous with museums, chapels, and moats if you are interested in military buffs. In the 17th century, the Spanish built the 2,300-ft. long Fortaleza de la Cabana to the south to defend the city.

Vedado and Beyond

One evening we drove west through Vedado past many beautiful art-deco mansions, museums and buildings that were crumbling from years of neglect on our way to the infamous Tropicana Cabaret and Club. The club is a distance from Havana's center on a 6-acre tropical garden estate known as Villa Mina located on a mountain side in Havana's Marianao neighborhood.

In 1939, the outdoor cabaret opened and became known as "Paradise Under the Stars". The cabaret featured well known entertainers including Xavier Cugat, Paul Robeson, Yma Sumac, Carmen Miranda, Nat King Cole, and Josephine Baker. Stars and entertainers frequenting the Tropicana included Édith Piaf, Ernest Hemingway, Jimmy Durante, Pier Angeli, Maurice Chevalier, Sammy Davis, Jr. and Marlon Brando. By 1946, the mob took over operations for the La Cosa Nostra and Tampa Family casino and business interests. The showgirls tended to be voluptuousness covered in sequins-and-feathers. This is still true today with a
3-hour series of conga songs, lights and elaborate Caribbean costumes. The scantily clad Tropicana chandelier dancer is still part of the show today. (Tropicana Show Havanna, 2017)

Cabaret Shows take place at 9 pm, Tuesday to Sunday, in the open-air Salon Bajo Las Estrellas (weather permitting). There is no air conditioning and it can be very uncomfortable if it is hot and humid as it was when I went. I found that the layout of the tables and seats made it difficult to see the show. I question whether it was worth spending $95 to sit at the back of the theater having to look around people to see everything. But with an extra $25 you could secure better seats closer to the stage. Would I go again, my answer is no. For $95 we got a glass of champagne, a bucket of ice, a bottle of Havana Rum to share, a can of cola and peanuts during the 3-hour show. After the first hour, the music was the same as the men and women came to stage in different costumes.

Bay of Pigs Museum at Playa Giron details the story of the ill-fated, CIA-sponsored operation to overthrow Castro in 1961. A Cuban Air Force Sea-Fury and both Soviet-era and American tanks from the battle will thrill military enthusiasts, and the exhibits provide an enlightening take on events from the Cuban government's perspective.

Varadero

This resort town hosts over a million people per year, mostly from Europe and Canada because of the large number of private hotels. There are 20 miles of beautiful beaches and crystal-clear water. The area has evolved into a paradise dream with mansions turned into museums, private homes turned into villas, accessible virgin cays and caves waiting to be explored and popular deep-sea fishing and dive sights. Due to restrictions on visitors from the United States, visits to beaches of Cuba are limited. Prior to the Cuban Revolution in 1959 visitors from the U.S. included famous people like Al Capone.

After the revolution many mansions of the rich and famous were many mansions were confiscated by the Cuban Government and were made into museums and government buildings.

Finca Vigia

Just outside of Havana in San Francisco de Paula is the estate of American Author Ernest Hemingway. On top of a hill you can see Havana in the distance from Finca Vigia or "lookout farm". His home was built in 1886 by a Spanish Architect Miguel Pascual y Baguer. Hemingway spent time on the estate sailing between Cuba and Miami on his boat "Pilar" from 1940 until 1960 when the Cuban Government took over control of the property and opened it to tourism and the public. After a short drive through the streets of the village surrounding the estate we drove up a hill and I immediately knew why he decided to make his home there. Fresh smelling air and beautiful groves of trees surrounded the home atop the hill. (Ernest Hemingway's Home in Cuba, 2015)

A father plays catch, national pass time, with his son just below the home owned by Hemingway. And, across the street you can see the homes inhabited by locals. Modest bungalows with their water supply and clothes lines above.

Starting at the base of the hill are the iron gates and road that meanders up to the top of the compound. The main house is airy and cooler than the surrounding property below.

The tower to the left of the house overlooks the City of Havana in the distance. On a clear day it's conceivable that you could even see the Florida Keys and Miami, Florida to the north.

The main house is surrounded by arbors with flowering plants and shrubs.

When I saw the gentleman below, I thought that "Papa" had returned to see all of the visitors to his beloved property.

If you happened to visit Hemmingway while he was still alive you might have found him one of three locations depicted below.

Each room had large open windows that allowed me to view Hemingway's favorite chair and liquors. It appears as if he just left the room to go to another part of the house.

0-5 Papa's favorite chair was an arm's length from his favorite drink and books.

0-6 While he was in the mood to write Hemmingway used the massive desk in his library.

0-7 Even Hemmingway's bed was close to shelves full of books.

0-8 Depicted here are the uniforms that Hemmingway wore while he was in the military.

Below the home is the footpath that leads to the pool where he entertained friends visiting him from the main land United States. In the changing room there were photographs of the rich and famous that visited the compound.

When he left the property for the last time, his boat named Pilar was put under shelter for visitors to see. The grave stones are markers for the burial of his pets.

Some visitors to the property decided to pay for a vintage ride while others bought something from the vendor at the bottom of the hill.

Cayo Santa Maria

The small island of Cayo Santa Maria is connected to the mainland of Cuba by a road and bridge to nearby Caibarién. Frequent visitors are the Canadians, British and Europeans who come to relax on the beautiful beaches and shop at all-inclusive resorts. The island is well known for its fishing lodges and bonefish and tarpon in the coastal flats.

Santa Clara

Santa Clara is the capital city of the province of Villa Clara located in the center of Cuba. The city is the home of a massive mausoleum dedicated to the revolutionary hero Che Guevara. In the center of the city is Parque

Hotel Habanilla (near Santa Clara) offers fishing for bass.

Vidal, a large park where locals meet each afternoon, Within the park is a statue of Marta Abreu. There are several places that you can visit within a short walk of the park including historical hotels like the Santa Clara Libre and the Gran Hotel, the former City Hall and the center for dance, the Colonia Española de Santa Clara Center. Train buffs may want to visit the Parque del Tren Blindado (AKA the Armored Train Park-Museum). The Catedral de Santa Clara de Asís or Saint Claire of Asis Cathedral is also a point of interest.

Cayo Coco

Cayo Coco is the largest resort area after Varadero filled with swamps and scrubland, beautiful beaches and a massive coral reef to the north. The area attracts divers and tourist from all over the world many flying directly into the international airport, the Jardines del Rey Airport. Coming from the mainland you will drive along the 17-mile road linking Cayo Coco to the mainland and cross the Perros Bay (Bahia de Perros); watch for wild flamingos that still live in the shallow water.

Camagüey

In 1528, the third largest city of Camagüey was settled by the Spaniards. Located in central Cuba the city is the capital of the Camagüey Province. While visiting Camagüey you may want to take a bicycle taxi city tour and visit with artists at the Casanova Pottery Studio or see vintage cars at the American Car Association or

In July 2008, Camagüey, the old town was designated a UNESCO World Heritage Site.

an art gallery or museum. Many visitors go to a movie theater or attend a performance by the Camagüey Ballet Company. If you're Hungry, there are plenty of restaurants and paladars in this city.

Holguín

In 1545, Captain Garcia Holguin a Spanish military officer discovered Holguin. Holguín is Cuba's the fourth largest city. Today you can fly into the Frank País International Airport (city code HOG) to visit the city if you don't want to drive. The area is surrounded by sandy beaches and pristine coral reefs that attract a variety of marine life. The city is known for its numerous parks, print shop, organ factory and baseball stadium. A visit to the Province Museum La Periquera, a science and history museum may be worth some time. On top Loma de la Cruz is a large crucifix. When you walk up the 450 stairs from the bottom of the hill you can see the entire city.

Mayabeque and Matanzas

On August 1, 2010 the Cuban National Assembly split the La Habana Province in half creating the Mayabeque Province and the Artemisa Province. The area is on the Bay of Matanzas on the northern coast of Cuba west of Varadero and only 56 miles from the City of Havana.

Matanzas, the City of Bridges, has 17 bridges that cross one of the three rivers: the Rio Yumuri, San Juan, and Canimar. Hence, locals refer to the city as the Venice of Cuba and the Athens of Cuba, La Atenas de Cuba for its poets. Matanzas is also the birthplace the danzón and rumba.

Gibara

On January 16, 1817, "the White Town" of Gibraltar was founded. In 2002, Gibara was designated a National Monument. Today the International Festival of Poor Cinema features a variety of films during that event. Visit Gibara and attend a workshop with local fisherman or learn how to make the mojito at a local paladar.

Baracoa

On November 27, 1492, Admiral Christopher Columbus discovered Baracoa. The city is an isolated location near the eastern tip of Cuba and is the oldest Spanish settlement in Cuba. When he landed he met the Taíno people, the original inhabitants of the island. Within several years many of the tribe died after being exposed to diseases brought over by the Spanish. The remaining descendants of the Taíno people have married into other races.

In the 16th and 17th centuries, Baracoa was a haven for illegal trade with the French and English. And in the early 19th century, the French came from Haiti and started growing coffee and cocoa. Later in the 19th century many independence fighters landed here including Antonio Maceo and José Martí. Both were instrumental in Cuba's independence from Spain in 1902.

Playa Larga

Cuba's Zapata Wetlands are located in the Zapata National Park, a UNESCO Biosphere Reserve and the largest wetlands in the Caribbean.

Cayo Largo

The small, limestone resort island of Cayo Largo del Suror Cayo Largo ("Long Cay"), is an island off the south coast. The 16-mile-long and 1.9-mile-wide pure white beaches make the island a very popular destination. The second largest island in the Canarreos Archipelago Cayo Largo is part of the special municipality of Isla de la Juventud. (Caayo Largo, 2017) It was formed by

> Cayo Largo is known for it's fishing lodges and bonefish and tarpon in the coastal flats.

marine organisms that build coral reefs. Today tourists visit the island to see the vibrant coral reefs and dive in the water off shore. On the northern coast there are groves of mangrove trees and salt pans and the water tends to be cloudy. To the south the water is so clear that you can see ocean floor. Divers encounter underwater caves, valleys and steep, gorgonian-encrusted walls, colorful tropical fish, sponges and coral reefs.

Naturalists enjoy the native wildlife found on the island including Cuba's tiny bee hummingbirds, flamingos, and iguanas. Sea turtles also nest on the beaches of the island. The island features museums with unique artifacts and exhibits. It is worthwhile to visit the cave at the Cueva de Punta del Este or aboriginal Sistine Chapel to see hundreds of historic pictographs. (Cuba Tourism Portal)

Cienfuegos

0-1 Statue to Bene Moré on the green in Cienfuegos.

Cienfuegos means "one hundred fires, cien meaning "one hundred", fuegos meaning "fires". The area was originally settled by Taino people of the Caribbean. When the French settled the area, it was known as the "Little Paris" of the Caribbean or the "Pearl of the South". It is the center for sugar, coffee, and tobacco trade. In 2005 Cienfuegos was listed as a UNESCO World Heritage Site citing Cienfuegos as the best extant example of early 19th century Spanish implementation in urban planning.

There are many famous people who called Cienfuegos their home including Benny Moré, the Cuban singer and Jazz Muscian and María Conchita Alonso.

While in Cienfuegos we took a walking tour of historic city center and attended a performance by the Cienfuegos Choir. You can also visit the Cienfuegos Botanical Garden or talk to tobacco rollers at a cigar factory.

Attractions

Old Mansions on the Coast

The mansion to the left has been turned into a government building. The Palacio de Valle (above right) a beautiful former palace that now houses a museum. The neo-gothic structure was built between 1913–1917.

Sports Stadium

0-2 Ball field in Cienfuegos

Cienfuegos fields a team in the Cuban National Series, the Cienfuegos Elefantes. Since joining the league in 1977–78, the best finish the Camaroneros have achieved is a 3rd place showing in the 2010–11 Cuban National Series. American Baseball greats Cristóbal Torriente, Joe Azcue, Yasiel Puig, José Abreu all hail from this area.

As we drove into the center we passed several parks and storefronts. The streets were almost devoid of cars and pedestrians even though it was the middle of the day.

Even though Cienfuegos is supposed to be a large city I didn't see much activity. There were vendors delivering goods some shoppers visiting the local stores.

The Business Zone

0-3 Photos of Fidel Castro could be seen throughout the city.

0-4 Private businesses used to have their quarters above the business. After the revolution the Cuban Government confiscated all buildings creating government run businesses below and public housing above.

0-5 Government barber shop / beauty parlor.

0-6 Industrious street vendors near Plaza de Armas

Parque José Martí – park in Plaza de Armas

0-7 Monument Dedicated to José Martí

Parque José Martí – park in Plaza de Armas

0-8 Plaza de Armas - Compass to the rest of the World.

0-9 City Hall

Parque José Martí – park in Plaza de Armas

Parque José Martí – park in Plaza de Armas

0-10 The Royal Palm is Cuba's National Tree

0-11 The only Arco de Triunfo in Cuba

0-12 Another beautiful building seen from the Plaza de Armas

The building on page 91 is being renovated. At one time it was a private residence. The Cuban Government is using tourist dollars to modernize buildings like this through the country. The woman at the bottom of the stairs of that building was even collecting 5CUCs for us to enter and take photographs.

0-13 Cathedral de la Purisma Concepción – cathedral with stained glass work, built 1833–1869.

0-14 Teattro Tomas Terry Opera House. It is near the Plaza de Armas

Trinidad

In 1514 the Spanish settled in Trinidad now known as "The Museum City of Cuba". In 1988 it was named a UNESCO World Heritage Site. Trinidad is known for its tobacco and sugar fields that created huge fortunes for the land owners in the 19th century. The city is located between the Sierra del Escambray mountains to the north and the Caribbean Ocean to the south. The picturesque town makes it one of the most photographed cities in Cuba including the Santísima Trinidad Cathedral and Convento de San Francisco. The city is very walkable with cobblestone streets flanked by pastel colored buildings with wrought-iron grilles. Trinidad's Plaza Mayor is an open-air museum of Spanish Colonial architecture with numerous colonial buildings, sugar mills, slave barracks, palaces and mansions of sugar barons. You might want to visit the workshop at Templo Yemaya as well as one of Trinidad's art galleries and museums including the Museo Histórico Municipal and the Museo de Arquitectura Trinitaria. If you have time then you should visit the Valle de los Ingenios or Valley of the Sugar Mills to see the ruins of 70 historic 19th century sugar mills located just outside the city. Here you can participate in including bass fishing in the Embalse Zaza.

Plaza Mayor and Iglesia y Convento de San Francisco (Bruyere, 2008)

Santiago de Cuba

Formed in 1515, Santiago de Cuba is Cuba's second-largest city and hottest city on the island because of its location and it's surrounded by rain forests. The city was plundered by French forces in 1553, and by British forces under Christopher Myngs in 1662. In addition to the French and British immigrants in the 18th and 19th centuries, Haitians came to settle after the slave revolt of 1791.

During my trip there the heat was intense and the humidity was equally as high. It was late July and the raunchy carnival "Festival del Caribe" or the Carnival had just finished. We saw the benches along the parade route that featured traditional conga music performed on the traditional pentatonic trumpet, called the trompeta china.

In the city there are multiple architectural styles, from Baroque to

neoclassical. Of special interest are the wooded parks, the steep streets, colonial buildings with huge windows and crowded balconies. Preserved historical treasures include the first home in the Americas, the first cathedral in Cuba, the first copper mine opened in the Americas and the first Cuban museum.

The city was wired for electricity on the streets we walked down had relatively few cars. It was interesting to note the architecture had a mix of old and new from the buildings below to the blue building that housed the Government Communication Center.

Santiago de Cuba Musica de Carnival – Coro Madrigalista

Some of Cuba's most famous musicians, including Compay Segundo, Ibrahim Ferrer and Eliades Ochoa (all of whom participated in the Buena Vista Social Club) and trova composer Nico Saquito (Benito Antonio Fernández Ortiz) were born in the city or in one of the villages surrounding it. They have contributed to the typical, country-like music of the city.

Furthermore, Santiago de Cuba is well known for its traditional dances, most notably son, from which salsa has been derived, and guaguancó, which is accompanied by percussion music only.

During our visit our group attended a performance at the Santiago de Cuba Musica where the group performed many of Cuba's traditional songs.

0-1 Everyone works in Cuba. I passed this pleasant woman as we walked back to Revolution Square.

0-2 Outside of the club we saw a musical group playing.

0-3 This museum that displays the extensive art collection of the Bacardi Rum family.

0-4 Courtyard of the Buena Vista Social Club

Santiago de Cuba's Revolution Square

The revolutionary hero, Frank País made Santiago de Cuba his home. The Cuban Revolution began July 26, 1953 with an attack by Fidel Castro a small group of rebels on the Moncada Barracks. After this poorly led attack, País began talking informally with young working people and students. This was the beginning of the formation of a very effective alliance of urban revolutionaries. As time passed the cells grew larger and became highly organized ensuring in the success of the Cuban Revolution. (Santiago de Cuba, 2017)

País' group prepared carefully all of the time collecting money, medical supplies and weapons. Their newsletter criticized Batista's censorship and the government reporting their version of the news.

On July 26th, 1955, País' revolutionaries joined with Castro's. País led the new group in Oriente province. In 1957, País was captured and shot after someone turned him into the Batista government.

By January 1, 1959, Fidel Castro stood on the balcony at Santiago de Cuba's city hall to proclaim victory. (Walter, 2008) (Cannon, 1981) (Cannon, Who was Frank Pais?, 2006) (Santiago de Cuba, 2017)

Below were two residents of the city who were spending some time in the park. Most residents were very slim compared to the visiting tourists.

0-5 Catedral de la Ciudad

San Juan Hill

On July 1, 1898 San Juan Hill was where Spanish troops faced their main defeat during the Spanish–American War. After capturing the surrounding hills, General William Rufus Shafter laid siege to the city. Spain later surrendered to the United States after Admiral William T. Sampson destroyed the Spanish Atlantic fleet just outside Santiago's harbor on July 3, 1898.

Changing of the Guards at Santa Efigenia Cemetery

Cuban poet, writer, and national hero, José Martí, is buried in Cementerio Santa Efigenia. Some of the photos in this section are of the tomb were built in his honor. Every day there is a changing of the guard. The cemetery is well manicured with workers cleaning the head stones and brass reliefs. It was interesting to noted that the Masons have a presence in the cemetery with tomb stones and monuments recognizing the presence of God, pre-revolution. Thankfully the Cuban Government hasn't decided to erase history by removing statues and all reference to God.

San Pedro de la Roca Castle

The local citadel of San Pedro de la Roca is inscribed on the UNESCO World Heritage List as "the most complete, best-preserved example of Spanish-American military architecture, based on Italian and Renaissance design principles."

0-6 San Pedro de la Roca Castle seen from the ship.

Pinar del Río

Pinar del Río is the 10th largest Cuban city. The Vinales Valley and Pinar del Río are a short drive from Havana. When visiting the area, you should stay overnight and walk to the top of the limestone mountain (mogotes) to see the amazing sunset and sunrise. The area smells like the tobacco fields that I grew up in Connecticut's Tobacco Valley. The Connecticut Valley is the only place in the world outside of Cuba that produces the same type of tobacco leaves used as wraps on cigars. (Pinar del Rio, 2017)

Cuba's finest cigars start out in the tobacco plantations of Cuba's westernmost province, Pinar del Río. The other reason to visit the area is the mountains or mogotes that surround the land growing the plant. The mogotes (rounded limestone mountains) are strung along flat plains. Here Cuban cowboys roam and small villages exist surrounded by mountain ranges and large tracts of tropical forests.

Pinar del Río factory tours may include a visit where and how Cuban cigars are made, or stop by the brandy plant taste the region's guava liqueur, Guayabita del Pinar. Or hike the scenic hiking trails that lead to mineral springs, the El Salto Waterfall, and historic coffee plantations. While in the area you could go to Soroa notable for its 750-orchid species. A visit to Pinar del Río's secluded beaches attracts visitors who wish to see caves, coral gardens and to dive in the crystal-clear water.

Why is a cedar sheet in my cigar box or tube? It is used to light your cigar. Traditional matches tend to give cigars a bad sulfur flavor, so you can just tear off of a strip of cedar, light the end of it, and use it to light your cigar.

The Valle de Viñales has been designated a World Heritage Site. It and two biosphere reserves – the Sierra del Rosario and Peninsula de Guanahacabibes give Pinar del Río more UNESCO-protected land than any other province in Cuba. (Webmaster, 2017)

Guantánamo

Guantánamo bay is well known to the U.S. public because it is the home of a U.S. naval base and terrorist detention center on the south-eastern side of the island. The base is well guarded and off limits to Cuban citizens and tourists. We saw the base as we passed the port of Caimanera on our ship.

Guantánamo is the boyhood home of Fidel and Raul Castro.

Guantánamo is also known for its cocoa farms and industry. This area still has a population of the semi-indigenous Guirito community who staff the Matachin Museum.

Everywhere that we went in Cuba to heard a coral group sing, the song "Guantanamera" was performed. It is one of the most well-known songs in the world and is a Cuban favorite. The title means woman from Guantánamo. Baby boomers from the United States recognize it because of the renditions sung by The Sandpipers in the 60s. A major tourist destination is Casa del Changui Baracoa where you can learn more about Cuba's music.

PLAN
How to Use QR Codes

Get more information on that hotel or cruise line here … then go!

If you can use "apps" on your cell phone, iPhone, Android or Window Device and it has a camera then you can download an application to read the codes in this book. Or, you can go to the back of the book and see the Web Links for each of the hotels and cruise lines that contributed recipes for the book. Point and Scan and you get information, a website or a phone number. Once you scan the code you can visit a website, call, and/or send an email right on your phone.

For example, when you scan the tag below you will get my contact information

Share & Save my information from the QR Code (above) to your contact list and follow me on Twitter. **Thanks, Bruce**

Get your reader and become more productive by following the next couple of steps:

- You can download the app for your:
  - o Android devices - Google Play
  - o Apple devices – AppStore
  - o Windows devices – Windows Apps
- Use one or more of the following search terms:
  - o QR code scanner
  - o Code scanner
  - o QR and barcode scanner
- Install one of the readers NOTE: some bar code scanners don't read QR Codes.

Cuban Vacation Options

Bruce Oliver has been to Cuba and has relationships with a variety of vendors who offer all types of travel options to Cuba from private tours, to cruise tours and land based tours. All of the companies that offer packages to Cuba have been vetted to make sure that they are reliable and we trust them. On the next couple of pages, you will be able to find the links to the packages that I offer.

Cuban Vacations

There are between five and eleven tour companies that offer a range of tours to Cuba each year. The cost varies based on the number of days and the type of vacation offered. The number of cities visited also varies depending upon the number of days. All programs follow the guidelines agreed to by the Department of Treasury and the Cuban Government and are subject to change at any time.

Current pricing can be obtained along with information about each organization by going to the following link (QR Code and Case Sensitive Short Address).

http://travelurl.net/CubanVacations

Cuban Cruise Tours

There are between two and seven cruise lines that offer stops at the various ports in Cuba each year. The cost varies based on the number of days and the cabin category. The number of cities visited also varies depending upon the number of days. All programs follow the guidelines agreed to by the Department of Treasury and the Cuban Government and are subject to change at any time.

Current pricing can be obtained along with information about each organization by going to the following link (QR Code and Case Sensitive Short Address)

http://travelurl.net/CubanCruiseTours

VISIT

1st Day of Visit: _____

Day Journal

2nd Day of Visit: _____

Day Journal

3rd Day of Visit: _____

Day Journal

4th Day of Visit: _____

Day Journal

5th Day of Visit: _____

Day Journal

6th Day of Visit: _____

Day Journal

7th Day of Visit: _____

COOK
FOOD & RECIPES

Cuban Food

Cuisine

Cuban farms grow a wide variety of beef, beans (frijoles), chicken (pollo), fruit, rice (arroz), root vegetables, and pork (cerdo, lechon) is often served. Cuban Cuisine is a blend of African, Caribbean, Spanish, and Taino, spices and techniques. Generally, Cuban dishes are not spicy but they aren't bland.

Cuban Citizens Food Supply

An Anonymous Cuban student told me that you will never find a malnourished Cuban therefore most people are very thin. There are some exceptions, my guides and some of the elites who have favor with the government. Each time my guides saw left over food on our tables they filled their plates and ate every leftover. I was told that there are three types of "grocery store" in Cuba:

- The Cuban government provides rationing stamps for the Cuban population to buy just enough food to keep them alive. These stores may or may not have fully stocked shelves every day and citizens need to come back multiple days to get items that are not available. If they run a "Paladar" they may have to go to a "private" store and pay out of pocket. Some Paladar proprietors need to shop several days to get enough food to host a backyard dinner once a week. These meals are usually frequented by foreign tourists.

- The next type of store requires citizens to pay out of pocket to purchase items that they couldn't get at government run stores. There are better quality items and more availability at this type of store.

- The last store is the most expensive and is usually the one that tourists are brought to. These stores have the best merchandise and the greatest availability. Citizens are able to make purchases at these establishments if they have enough money left out of their government stipend (roughly $20 U.S.).

Grocery Store Photographs

Photographs Courtesy of Linda Oster-Safier

Linda told me that she shot the following photographs at a food store that their guide brought her group to during her visit. You may be surprised to see how dirty the store is as well as the low number of items that are available. Some of the vegetables haven't even been washed. Would you eat the meat in the photograph on page 120? There was no refrigeration and the temperature was over 80 degrees.

Photographs Courtesy of Linda Oster-Safier

Traditional Cuban Breakfast

Breakfast is a light meal consisting of bread and butter, coffee with (warm) milk (café con leche), fresh fruits and melon, (ensalada de frutas), fried eggs (huevos fritos), mango, and pineapple. If you stay in a premium hotel you will also be served cheese and ham.

Traditional Cuban Lunch and Dinner

Common dishes are:

- Chicken and Rice - (Pollo con arroz) often served with plantains and a sauce of black beans.

- Picadillo - minced beef meat with a sauce of tomatoes, green peppers, onion and garlic.
- Rice and Black Beans - (Arroz y frijoles negros)
- Roasted Pork and Rice - (Lechon asado con arroz)

Cuban farms produce most if not all of the produce and ingredients used in their recipes.

While in Cuba my guide told me, urban farms use citizens who refuse to work. He said: "After Russian money dried up in 1989, the government, in their wisdom, realized that the country doesn't produce anything. So, they began to arrest people who refuse to work and sentence them to a one (1) year of hard labor on a 'work farm' (I call it a 'chain gang', now illegal in the United States.)."

When asked what happens to Citizens who refuse to work the second time he said second offenders are sentenced to five (5) years of hard labor.

- Ropa Vieja - meat stew of shredded beef simmered with tomatoes, green peppers, onion and garlic.

(Cuban Food, 2017) (Best Food in Cuba, 2016) (Best Food in Cuba, 2016)

Cuban Fast Food

There is a growing tendency to fast food in the country. At the street stalls, called "Kiosko", cheap pizza and Cuban sandwiches are sold.

At the food chain "EL RAPIDO" you can eat fried chicken. Watch out with this street foods, hygiene is not their strong point.

Pizza is popular, made of soft bread, cheese, toppings and sauce with onion, but the quality cannot be compared to Western standards.

In the cheap eateries, you can eat besides pizza, spaghettis with cheese (or something, they call 'cheese'). "Pizzeria Parque Central" in Central Havana is a popular and cheap pizza restaurant.

Consider for quality food, the fruits from the fresh products markets, called "agromercados", like mercado de Cuatro Caminos Maximo Gomez street 256 Havana Centro. These fruits are of excellent quality and without artificial fertilizers straight from the urban farms. (Cuban Food, 2016)

COOK
Cuban Sandwich

The 8-12-inch Cuban sandwich consists of roasted pork, glazed ham, Swiss cheese, mustard, and sliced dill pickles on top Cuban bread that's lightly oiled with olive oil and grilled lightly on a non-grooved grill*. In some quarters the Italians add salami to the mixture. Other ingredients may vary as well. American Cubanos often contain lettuce, tomatoes, mayonnaise, or aioli. According to Andrea Gonzmart Williams, fifth-generation co-owner of Tampa, Florida's Columbia Restaurant: "Layering all of the ingredients evenly and in the correct order" is the key to creating the ideal Cuban sandwich, "From the bottom to the top: ham, roast pork, salami, Swiss cheese, pickle chips and yellow mustard on the top half of the bread."

NOTE: The non-grooved grill is called a plancha, which is similar to a panini press. The grill both heats and compresses the sandwich. You should keep the sandwich in the press until the bread surface is slightly crispy and the cheese is melted. When done the sandwich is cut into diagonal halves then it is served.

Cuban Paella.

Although Spain is the traditional destination for paella, Cuba offers its own version made with ham, chicken, mussels, chorizo, shrimp, scallops, and lobster. (Red paella with mussels.jpg, 2017)

A very traditional Cuban dish and originally from Spain, this dish is a seafood paradise, including the best ingredients which give it a very zestful taste. It is very time consuming, and takes several hours to cook, but the results are well worth it!

Ingredients Serving Size: 8:

8 unskinned chicken pieces	**8 minced garlic gloves**
1/2 cup cooked Chorizo, sliced into 1/4-inch pieces	**2 teaspoons salt**
	1 chopped large onion
1 lobster tail (meat removed and cut into small pieces)	**1 chopped green bell pepper**
	1 chopped red bell pepper
1 lb. medium-sized scallops	**3/4 cup red wine**
1 lb. medium peeled and deveined shrimp	**3 cups parboiled rice**
	2 tbsp. olive oil
1 dozen washed clams	**5 cups water**
1 dozen cleaned mussels	**2 packs Saffron**
4 cups chicken broth	**1/2-pound frozen green peas**

Directions

You will need a paellera or large covered pot. Heat the olive oil over medium-high in the paellera. Lightly brown the chicken pieces on both sides, then place the sausage (Chorizo) while the chicken is frying. Once the chicken is browned on both sides, remove the chicken and sausage and place them in a large bowl. Next place the onions, green bell peppers and garlic in the paellera and sauté until the onion is translucent.

Add the salt, chicken broth, and wine to the paellera. Cover and cook for 5 minutes. Then add the chicken, sausage, rice, water, peas and saffron to the paellera. Stir in all the ingredients well. Cover, reduce the heat to medium-low and simmer for half an hour. The rice should be tender at this point.

While the rice is cooking, prepare the seafood. Steam the clams and mussels until they open, and set aside. Heat extra olive oil in a large pan, and sauté a few extra sausage pieces in the olive oil. Remove the sausage, then sauté the shrimp, pieces of lobster, and scallops for a couple of minutes. Remove the seafood, and mix into the paellera, stirring all of the seafood into the rice.

Remove paellera from stove, and place in the oven (preheat to 350 degrees). Bake for 15 minutes to allow the flavors to blend. Allow to cool for 5 minutes and serve warm. You may also garnish with sliced red bell peppers. Enjoy!

The Frita

Known as the Cuban hamburger, the frita is a patty of seasoned ground beef — sometimes mixed with chorizo — topped with crunchy shoe string known as the Cuban hamburger, the frita is a patty of seasoned ground beef — sometimes mixed with chorizo — topped with crunchy shoe string fries, all sandwiched in between a Cuban bun. Some places even add a fried egg.

The original Cuban Frita is a pork patty and a seasoned ground beef mixed with chorizo that's served on Cuban bread topped with shoestring potatoes. Some also make it with a spiced ketchup sauce, onions, and lettuce. A similar dish served in South Florida is topped with the shoestring potatoes on Cuban bread is called pan con bistec (bistec de palomilla).

Often people eat it with a drink of batido de trigo, a puffed wheat milk shake. (Frita, 2018)

Corn on the cob.

Corn on the cob is done a little differently in Cuba. The corn is grilled, rolled in cojita cheese, sprinkled generously with chili powder, and finished off with some lime juice, making for a richer and spicier taste.

Cuban Cod and Black Bean Salad

Ingredients

¾ lb. firm white fillets (cod, rockfish, snapper, orange roughy, lingcod, pike)

vegetable cooking spray

1 clove garlic; minced

1 tbsp. + 4 tsp lime juice; divided

¼ cup vegetable oil

½ tsp ground cumin

¼ tsp red pepper flakes or cayenne pepper

¼ tsp salt

1 can black beans (15 oz can) - drained and rinsed

1 large orange

4 cups torn romaine lettuce

Directions

1. Place in even layer (tucking under thin ends) on broiler pan coated with vegetable cooking spray.
2. Combine garlic and 2 teaspoons lime juice; spread on.
3. Broil about 4 inches from heat about 5 minutes or until just flakes when tested with a fork.
4. Transfer to a dish and let cool 10 minutes.
5. Combine oil, remaining 1 tablespoon and 2 teaspoons lime juice, cumin, pepper flakes and salt in a small jar.
6. Shake well and pour 1 tablespoon over.
7. Meanwhile, peel orange, cut into ½-inch slices and separate into segments.
8. Combine with black beams and remaining dressing.
9. Drain, break into large chunks and remove any bones.
10. Add to orange mixture and toss gently.
11. Cover and refrigerate 2 hours or up to 24 hours.
12. Serve over romaine.

Churro
Ingredients:
1 cup flour of flour.

½ teaspoon salt.
1 tablespoon butter.
1 cup milk.
oil for deep frying.
Preparation:

Place the milk, butter, and salt in a pot and bring to a boil. Remove from the heat.
Add flour, mixing quickly and continuously with a wooden spoon.
Place the dough in a cookie gun or mold to make churros and extrude them into the hot, fryer oil.
Cut them with scissors when they are the correct length.
Sprinkled with sugar, or fill them with sweet caramel, Guava or another fruit filling.
NOTE: You will need a churro making machine and a deep fryer to make this recipe.

"A Churro is a fried-dough pastry, predominantly choux (light pastry dough) based snack. Churros are popular in Spain, Portugal, France, the Philippines, Ibero-America and the Southwestern United States. In Spain, churros can either be thin (and sometimes knotted) or long and thick. They are normally eaten for breakfast dipped in hot chocolate, dulce de leche or café con leche." (Churros, 2016)

If you don't want to make these tasty treats, then try going to Costco and buy them. They are just as good without the bother.

Croquetas

Ingredients (Makes 20 to 24 croquetas)**:**

8 ounces smoked ham, excess fat or rind trimmed, cubed.
1 tablespoon Dijon mustard.
4 tablespoons unsalted butter.
1/2 cup minced shallots.
2 tablespoons plus 1/2 cup unbleached all-purpose flour.
1 cup whole milk.
1/2 cup grated hard yellow Gruyere or Emmental cheese.
1/8 teaspoon freshly ground nutmeg.
Pinch of sweet paprika (optional).
Kosher salt and freshly ground pepper.
2 well beaten large eggs.
1 1/2 cups finely ground dried breadcrumbs.
Coconut oil, Sunflower oil or Regular Olive Oil suitable for high
temperature deep frying.

Preparation: (Cooking Channel TV, 2016)

Combine ham and mustard in a food processor and pulse until it forms a smooth paste.

Melt the butter in a heavy saucepan over medium-low heat. Add the shallots and sauté until translucent. Add 2 tablespoons of the flour and cook, stirring

> Many people know this dish as Croquettes but in Cuba they're known as Croquetas. It is popular in southeastern Cuba due to the French influence. In France and much of the world it is very popular as a fast food. The word croquette came from the French word "croquer" meaning "to crunch" (Croquettes, 2016)

constantly until well blended but not browned, about 2 minutes. In the meantime, gently heat the milk to a gentle simmer but do not let it boil. Gradually stir the milk in to the saucepan, whisking constantly to eliminate clumps. Stir until the sauce has thickened and the whisk leaves trace marks in the surface, about 5 minutes. Stir in cheese and season with salt, pepper, nutmeg and sweet paprika. Remove from heat. Add the pureed ham and mix until well combined.

Bring to room temperature. Pour the mixture in a shallow bowl or lined baking sheet. Cover with plastic wrap and refrigerate until set, at least 1 hour.

Lay out the remaining 1/2 cup of flour, beaten eggs, and breadcrumbs in separate mixing bowls. Scoop out 1 heaping tablespoon of the béchamel mixture and roll each croqueta in the flour to coat, shaking off the excess flour. Dip into the egg mixture with a fork or slotted spoon, allowing excess to drip off, and then roll in breadcrumbs. They should be well coated so the filling doesn't leak when cooked.

Add about 3-inches of oil to a large, deep pot. Heat over medium-high heat to 365 degrees F. Working in batches, carefully add the croquetas a few at a time. Do not crowd them or the temperature of the oil will drop. Gently turn until brown on all sides, about 2 minutes. Remove with a slotted spoon and drain on paper towels or re-purposed grocery paper bags. Bring the oil back up to the correct temperature in between batches. Serve immediately.

Plátanos Maduros.

Plantains are a member of the banana family, but higher in starch and lower in sugar. The sweet fried "banana" is a staple in Cuban cooking and are served as a side dish in just about every Cuban restaurant.

Platanos maduros are caramelized plantains that have been lightly fried so that they're browned, sticky, and sweet. By Three Guys from Miami

Ingredients (4 Servings):

**3 large ripe, nearly rotten, plantains that have very black skin
2/3 cup vegetable oil, enough to cover half the plantains in the pan
Preparation:
Peel and diagonal cut the plantains into one-inch thick slices.
Heat the oil until medium hot.
Fry the pieces a minute or two per side.
Reduce heat to low and continue cooking.
Turn occasionally until they are brown and caramelized.**
Variation: Some people like to lightly roll the plantains in white or brown sugar before frying.

Chicharrónes.

Chicharrónes are crispy fried pork rinds, which can be made either from pork skin or fried pork belly. Chicharrón may also be made from chicken, mutton, or beef."

Moros y Cristianos

The meat and potatoes of Cuban cuisine, white rice and black beans is a common dish known in Spanish as moros y cristianos.

Pan Frito

Ingredients

¼ cup olive oil for sautéing

3 cloves garlic, crushed with a pinch of salt

1 tablespoon chopped fresh parsley

1 loaf Cuban bread sliced into one-inch thick slices (you may substitute French bread)

lemon juice to taste

freshly grated Parmesan cheese (optional)

Directions

1. Slice the bread into one-inch slices.
2. Place the rounds on a cutting board and use a heavy frying pan or bacon press to compress them slightly.
3. Heat the oil in a large sauté pan.
4. Toss in the crushed garlic and parsley and sauté for one minute only, stirring constantly.
5. Add the bread and sauté over medium heat until the bread is browned on both sides.
6. Just before removing the toast from the pan, sprinkle the slices with a **little** fresh lemon juice.
7. Serve immediately.

Directions

1. Slice the bread into one-inch slices.
2. Place the rounds on a cutting board and use a heavy frying pan or bacon press to compress them slightly.
3. Heat the oil in a large sauté pan.
4. Toss in the crushed garlic and parsley and sauté for one minute only, stirring constantly.
5. Add the bread and sauté over medium heat until the bread is browned on both sides.
6. Just before removing the toast from the pan, sprinkle the slices with a **little** fresh lemon juice.
7. Serve immediately.

Ropa Vieja – "Cuban Beef Stew"

Ingredients (Serves: 6):

For the meat:

2 pounds of flank steak, cut into pieces.

2 sprigs of fresh spearmint.
½ small bunch fresh flat-leaf parsley, stems removed.
4 large garlic cloves, peeled and crushed.
1 teaspoon whole black peppercorns.
1 teaspoon salt.
1 teaspoon whole allspice.
½ teaspoon whole cloves.
2 dried bay leaves.
1 large carrot, peeled and cut into chunks.
½ small red cabbage, quartered.
For the Ropa Vieja:

For the vegetables you can substitute a package of frozen mixed vegetables containing carrots, peas, string beans, tomatoes.

Ropa Vieja (Spanish translation "old clothes") tastes better than it sounds. I had it at a restaurant at the base of the UNESCO World and heritage site of Castello De San Pedro De La Rocca, a coastal fortress locally known as El Morro on a hill above Santiago de Cuba. In the states we would call it beef stew. In Cuba it is usually served with rice, as I had it, or over tortillas.

1½ cups canned crushed tomatoes or tomato puree.
1 large thinly sliced yellow onion.
1 large thinly sliced green bell pepper (no seeds).
1 cup of roasted and sliced red bell peppers.
A small bunch of chopped fresh parsley
¼ cup olive oil.
4 large peeled garlic cloves.
½ teaspoon ground black pepper.
1 teaspoon salt.
1 large pinch ground cloves.
½ teaspoon ground allspice.
1 dried bay leaf.
¼ cup dry white wine.

Preparation:

1. Place all the ingredients for the stew meat in a 5-quart pot with 6 cups of water.
2. Bring to a boil, reduce the heat, and simmer, covered, 1½ - 2 hours, until the beef is tender.
3. Remove from the heat and allow the beef to cool in the broth.
4. When cool, remove the beef and shred by hand.
5. Set the shredded beef aside.

6. Also set aside a ½ cup of the broth, reserving the remaining broth for future use.
7. To prepare the Ropa Vieja, heat the olive oil in a skillet over medium heat.
8. Add the green bell pepper and onion then sauté until the onion is soft.
9. Mash or use a blender to blend the garlic, black pepper, salt, cloves and allspice to a paste.
10. Add the paste to the skillet and continue to cook for another couple of minutes until fragrant.
11. Add the bay leaf, extra broth, tomato and wine and return to a simmer.
12. Stir in the shredded beef and lower the heat to low.
13. Cook in a covered pot for another 15-20 minutes.
14. Finally, stir in the sliced roasted red bell peppers.
15. Adjust seasonings to taste.

Huevos Habaneros
AKA Havana Style Eggs

"Sofrito" Sauce Ingredients (Serves 4):

1/4 cup pure Spanish olive oil.
1 small onion, finely chopped.
1 small green bell pepper, finely chopped.
2 cloves garlic, finely chopped.
1 cup canned tomatoes, drained and chopped (or prepared tomato sauce).
1/2 cup pimiento, drained.
2 tablespoons dry sherry.
Fresh ground black pepper to taste.

Eggs Ingredients:

8 large eggs.
4 tablespoons sweet salted butter.
salt and fresh black pepper to taste.
1 tablespoon chopped parsley to garnish.

Preparation:

1. Preheat oven to 350.
2. In a skillet over low heat, heat the oil until it is fragrant.
3. Next cook the onion, bell pepper, and garlic, stirring, until tender, this usually takes 8 to 10 minutes.
4. Add the tomatoes, pimientos, and sherry, cook until thickened, 15 minutes, and season with salt and pepper.
5. Lightly oil 4 "*ramekins*" and divide the sofrito sauce among them.
6. For each dish, break two eggs into a saucer, slide them on top of the tomato mixture, and drizzle with 1 tablespoon melted butter.
7. Bake for about 10 to 12 minutes until the whites are set and the yolks are still soft.
8. Sprinkle with salt, pepper, and parsley.
9. Serve immediately from the baking dishes.

> **A ramekin is a small baking dish.** The term is derived from French *ramequin*, originally a cheese- or meat-based dish baked in a small mold. (Ramekin, 2016)

Vaca frita.

Related to ropa vieja, vaca frita means fried cow, and features beef marinated in lime, garlic, and salt, then seared until crispy.

"Vaca Frita (literally "Fried Cow") is a Cuban dish consisting of fried and shredded beef marinated in lime, garlic and salt then seared into a crispy texture. It is often topped with sautéed onions and served with rice and black beans.

Absolutely wonderful! Simmered beef marinated overnight in lime, lemon and garlic, then sautéed with onion until slightly crispy (then I like to blast it with more fresh-squeezed lime juice!). The technique is almost like making homemade roast beef hash (without the potato). Prep time includes marinating beef overnight. Cook time is combination of two days (simmering of beef, then sautéing). (Raichlen, 1993) (20 dishes everyone should try in Cuba, 2017)

Ingredients Serves 4:

2 lbs. roast (I use a sirloin roast for less fat, but you can use chuck roast).
3 bay leaves.
4 tablespoons fresh lime juice.
4 tablespoons fresh lemon juice.
2 cloves garlic, finely minced.
4 tablespoons olive oil.

1⁄2 large onion, thinly sliced.
fresh parsley, as desired.

Preparation

1. Simmer roast with bay leaves in a Dutch oven on the stove until tender, about 1 to 1-1/2 hours.
2. Cool at room temperature; reserve cooking water for another use if you wish.
3. When beef is cool, shred and place in a glass container.
4. Combine lime juice, lemon juice and garlic; mix into meat.
5. Season with salt and pepper and marinate overnight.
6. (The sirloin roast is excellent at "soaking up" the juices!) Next day, remove meat from marinade, squeezing excess liquid (if you need to; I normally don't) and fry in a large skillet in olive oil until slightly brown, about 10 to 15 minutes.
7. Add thin onion slices and parsley and cook for another 10 to 15 minutes, until onion is tender and meat is well-browned.
8. Squeeze more lime juice on meat and serve over rice.

Cuban Flan
AKA – "Flan de Coco y Ron"

Ingredients:

1-1/2 cup sugar, divided.
5 large egg yolks.
3 large whole eggs.
1-3/4 cups coconut milk.
1 cup milk.
3 tablespoons dark rum (Santiago de Cuba 5-year reserve if you have it).

> **A traditional Cuban dessert is the Flan.** Think of it as a custard or version of a Crème Brule.

Preparation:

1. Heat oven to 325°. Have ready a 9" round-glass pie plate.

2. Place a clean kitchen towel in bottom of shallow baking pan large enough to hold pie dish.
3. Fill baking pan with enough boiling water to come halfway up sides of dish; transfer baking pan to oven.
4. Place 3/4 cup sugar in a heavy-bottomed, medium skillet.
5. Place over medium-high heat; cook until sugar begins to melt, swirling pan.
6. Cook until melted and medium-dark brown, about 5 minutes.
7. Remove from heat; pour caramelized sugar into pie dish.
8. Swirl dish until sugar evenly coats bottom; let cool.
9. In a large bowl, whisk together remaining 3/4 sugar, salt, egg yolks, and whole eggs until combined.
10. Pour into pie dish.
11. Transfer to hot-water bath in oven. Bake 45-50 minutes.
12. Refrigerate at least 4 hours.
13. When ready to serve, run a knife between flan and pie dish.
14. Place a serving dish on top of flan and invert.

U.S. Customs allows U.S. Citizens to bring back any amount of Cuban Rum. There is no longer a dollar amount.

15. Slice, and garnish with any remaining syrup. (Coconut and Rum Flan - Flan de Coco, 2017)

Cuban Tamales.

The biggest difference between Cuban tamales and Mexican tamales is that in Cuban tamales, the meat (usually pork) is mixed in with the dough of the tamale, instead of being used as a filling. Cubans also use field corn to make their tamales, which is less sweet and mealier than the corn you'll find in the US.

A tamale (tamal in Spanish, tamalli in Nahuatl) is a traditional Mesoamerican dish made of masa (a starchy dough, usually corn-based), which is steamed in a banana leaf or corn husk. Throw away the wrap pior to eating. Tamales can be filled with cheeses, chilies, fruits, meats, vegetables, or any preparation to your taste. Both the cooking liquid and filling may be seasoned. (Tamales, 2017)

Tamales originated in Mesoamerica as early as 8000 to 5000 BC. Aztec and Maya civilizations, as well as the Olmeca and Tolteca before them, used tamales as portable food, often to support their armies, but also for hunters and travelers.

The diversity of native languages in Mesoamerica led to several local words for the tamal, many of which remain in use. The Spanish singular of tamales is tamal. The English word "tamale" differs from the Spanish word by having a final vowel.
(Word Reference, 2016)

Unlike traditional Latin culture, Cuban's enjoy tamales throughout the entire year without a need for a celebration or family gathering. A variety of tamale recipes exits, but Cuban tamales have their own distinct taste. Typically made with pork, the corn husk wrapped tamales have a milder taste. A lot of preparation time goes into make tamales, but the tamales are well worth the wait. After preparation, the tamales can be stored in the freezer to enjoy later. (Hoyer, 2008)

Ingredients

1 ½ lbs. pork.
Water.
2 peeled garlic cloves.
1 tbsp. vinegar.
3 cups fresh corn.
¾-cup butter.
2 ½ cups chicken broth.
2 ½ cups masa harina.
Olive oil.
1 large chopped onion.
1 chopped green pepper.
5 minced garlic cloves.
3 oz. tomato paste.
½-cup warm water.
1 juiced lemon.
1 tsp. salt.
½ tsp. ground black pepper.
Corn-husks.
Butcher's string.

Preparation

1. Use pork with plenty of fat such as country style pork ribs. Cut the pork into small pieces at least 2 inches thick and 3 inches long.
2. Place the pork in a large saucepan. Add enough water to cover the meat. Place two peeled garlic cloves and 1 tbsp. of vinegar into the saucepan.

3. Put the saucepan on the stove-top under high heat. Bring the mixture to a boil, and then reduce the heat to allow it to simmer. Allow the mixture to simmer until all the water boils away. Continue to fry the pork until brown but not crispy.

4. Remove the pork from the saucepan. Trim off excess fat with a knife, and break the pork up into small pieces. Add the corn to a food processor with butter. Blend until the corn creates a coarse mixture with visible corn kernels. Try not to blend the corn too long or it will become mushy.

5. Remove the corn from the processor. Add 2 ½ cups chicken broth and 2 cups of masa harina to the ground corn. A mixture made with corn meal and lime, or you can purchase masa harina at your local specialty grocery store.

6. Place olive oil in a saucepan. Add just enough olive oil to cover the bottom of the pan. One the oil begins sizzling, add the chopped onion, minced garlic and green peppers. Cook until the onions and peppers become soft.

7. Add the tomato paste and ½-cup warm water to the frying pan. Simmer the mixture for 10 minutes.

8. Add the pork, vegetables and corn mixture into a large cooking pot. Add the lemon juice and blend the ingredients. Add salt and pepper to taste. Cook the entire mixture on low heat until it thickens, which typically occurs after 20 minutes. Add broth to keep the mixture pliable, but make sure that it stays stiff.

9. Remove the pot from the heat and allow it to cool. Soak the corn husks in warm water for 30 minutes. Remove two corn husks and overlap them on a flat surface. Place the corn mixture in the center of the corn husks.

10. Fold the corn husks over the filling using a short fold with top and bottom ends. Fold the husks over the long way from the ends until the two sides meet in the center and cover the short folds. Tie the Cuban tamale with butcher's string.

11. Place 2 inches of water in the bottom of a pot. Stand the tamales up in the pot and cover it with a lid. Bring the water to a boil, and then reduce the heat to allow them to steam for 2 hours. Do not let the water dry up completely in the pot. Consume the tamales immediately. Store any extra tamales in the freezer.

Lechón Asado (Cuban Roast Pork)

Ingredients:

First, make the mojo marinade.

15 cloves garlic, minced
2 teaspoons salt
2 cups orange juice
1 cup lemon juice
1 cup lime juice
1 cup onion, chopped
1 teaspoon oregano
1 cup olive oil
2 pounds boneless pork shoulder or loin of pork

Preparation:

1. Mix all ingredients together in a bowl or container. Add the pork and let marinate 4 to 5 hours or overnight.
2. Preheat oven to 325 degrees F. Place the pork and some marinade in a baking dish. Slowly roast the pork in the oven until the internal temperature of the meat reaches 155 degrees F. Don't let the meat dry out; spoon more marinade over it if needed.
3. Remove from oven and let the pork rest for 10 minutes before slicing.

Cuban-style Roast Suckling Pig

Ingredients

juice of 20 limes, strained
juice of 8 oranges, strained
4 large heads garlic
1 cup minced fresh oregano leaves
3 tablespoons ground cumin
4 cups roughly chopped cilantro leaves
1 tablespoon parsley leaves
5 tablespoons salt
1 whole suckling pig (12 to 15 pounds), split and washed

Directions

1. Place pig, belly down, into a large deep roasting pan.
2. Thoroughly rub pig with marinade.
3. Place in refrigerator overnight, basting occasionally.
4. Preheat oven to 275°F.
5. Pour off excess marinade from pan.
6. Cover pig's ears, snout and tail with aluminum foil.
7. Prop mouth open with 1½ inch ball of foil.

8. Place in oven and cook for about 4½ hours (20 minutes per pound) or until internal temperature reads 160°F.
9. Baste with marinade every 30 minutes.
10. If pig starts to get too dark while cooking, cover with aluminum foil.

Cuban Midnight Sandwich

Meaning midnight in Spanish, a medianoche is like a Cuban sandwich and is commonly served in Havana's nightclubs after midnight as well as many Cuban communities in the United States. Unlike a Cuban sandwich, there is no mayo on a medianoche; it's just ham, pork, cheese, and pickles pressed between sweet egg bread.

A medianoche consists of roast pork, ham, mustard, Swiss cheese, and dill pickles. It is a close cousin to the Cuban sandwich, the chief difference being that a medianoche is made on soft, sweet egg dough bread like Challah rather than on crustier Cuban bread. Like the Cuban sandwich, the medianoche is typically warmed in a press before eating. (A Taste of Cuba, 2017) (Classic Cuban Midnight (Medianoche) Sandwich Recipe, 2017)

Ingredients (Serves 4):

1 lb. thinly sliced cooked ham.
1 lb. thinly sliced fully cooked pork.
1 lb. sliced swiss cheese.
1 cup dill pickle slices.
1⁄2 cup mayonnaise.
1⁄4 cup prepared mustard.
2 tablespoons melted butter.
4 sweet bread rolls.

Preparation:

Split the sandwich rolls in half, and spread mustard and mayonnaise liberally onto the cut sides. On each sandwich, place and equal amount of Swiss cheese, ham and pork in exactly that order. Place a few pickles onto each one, and put the top of the roll onto the sandwich. Brush the tops with melted butter.

Press each sandwich in a sandwich press heated to medium-high heat. If a sandwich press is not available, use a large skillet over medium-high heat, and press the sandwiches down using a sturdy plate or skillet. Some indoor grills may be good for this also. Cook for 5 to 8 minutes, keeping sandwiches pressed. If using a skillet, you may want to flip them once for even browning. Slice diagonally and serve hot.

Pulpeta.

Pulpeta is the Cuban equivalent to meatloaf, but instead of being cooked in the oven, the mix of seasoned ground beef and ham is cooked on the stove, and there are hard boiled eggs on the inside.

Ingredients (should serve 6):

3/4lb. of ground beef.
1/4lb. of cooked ground ham.
20 olives.
4 eggs.
3 boiled eggs.
2 tablespoons of olive oil.
2 cups of cracker meal.
1 teaspoon each of oregano and cumin.
1 tablespoon of minced garlic.
1/2 a teaspoon of minced garlic.
1/4 of a teaspoon of pepper.
salt to taste.

For the sauce, combine:

2 tablespoons of tomato sauce.
1/2 a teaspoon of minced garlic.
1/4 of a teaspoon of oregano.
1/4 of a teaspoon of ground bay leaves.
1/2 a cup of cooking white wine.

Preparation:

Without doubt, meatloaf ranks up there as one of the world's most popular dishes – and in Cuba they feel no different. To prepare Cuban meatloaf – or pulpeta as it is known locally – you need to mix your ham and beef together with two well beaten eggs. Add salt, pepper, onion, garlic and oregano to flavor. Mix these up well and add enough cracker meal so that the meat contents hold their shape. Once you have this, you can form the contents into a large loaf-like shape. You then need to open the loaf by cutting across it, when you can then insert three hard boiled eggs and a line of olives down both sides. Close the loaf tightly, and then roll your loaf in the remaining two well beaten eggs. Add the remaining cracker meal. Place your loaf in a large skillet and brown the loaf in some pre-heated heated oil. Once you have a browned loaf, you need to prepare the sauce to go with the loaf. In Cuba this sauce is known as the salsa (like the dance), which you pour over the loaf and leave to simmer at 250 degrees Fahrenheit for three-quarters of an hour. Make sure to look in on the loaf and turn every now and then (probably not more than twice). Once the meatloaf has been well baked, allow the loaf to cool before slicing and serving.

Arroz con Pollo Cubano

Description

Somehow, the English translation "Cuban Chicken with rice" just doesn't do this exotic dish justice. Serve with salad, garlic bread, and wine, and you'll have a feast. Note that saffron is often less expensive if you purchase it at an oriental or other ethnic specialty market. You can make this dish a day ahead and reheat it. (If you double or triple the recipe, reduce the amount of water).

Ingredients Serves 4.

1 frying chicken, cut in serving pieces
1 onion, chopped
2 cloves garlic, minced
1 cup olive oil
6 oz canned tomatoes
6 cups water
1 bay leaf
2 tbsp salt
1 lb raw rice
1 pinch saffron
1 green pepper, cut in strips
2 pimentos, cut in strips
½ pkt frozen peas, cooked to almost tender

Directions

1. Preheat oven to 350°F.
2. Fry chicken with onion and garlic in oil until brown.
3. Add tomatoes and water; bring to a boil and cook 5 minutes.
4. Add bay leaf, salt, rice, saffron, and green pepper.
5. Place in 8" x 10" casserole; bake 20 to 30 minutes, stirring at least twice.
6. When water has been absorbed and chicken is fork tender, garnish with peas and pimientos.

Cuban Style Ribs
with Guava Glaze Costillitas

Costillitas are baby back ribs with a Cuban twist: The ribs are marinated and served with a mix of sour orange juice, lime juice, oregano, garlic, and olive oil, making for a sweet, tangy taste.

Ingredients (Serves 4 to 6):

2 - 3 racks of ribs (4 - 6 lbs.).
2 cups packed light brown sugar.
Juice of 2 lemons (Reserve the rind).
Juice of 2 limes (Reserve the rind).
2 Tbsp. ground allspice.
5 garlic.
cloves, crushed.
1 medium onion, sliced.
1 tsp kosher salt.
2 cups of water.

Guava Glaze

½ cup guava jelly.
½ cup packed light brown sugar.
Juice of 1 lime.
1 tsp apple cider vinegar.
1 tsp ground cumin.
½ tsp kosher salt.

Ribs

Remove white membrane from back of ribs. Cut rack in half if desired. In a 3-quart saucepan over medium heat, combine brown sugar, lemon juice, lemon rinds, lime juice, lime rinds, allspice, garlic, onion, salt and water. Cook for 3 - 5 minutes or until sugar is completely dissolved.

If using oven, preheat to 300F otherwise oil the grill racks. Preheat grill with all burners on high for 10 - 12 minutes with lid closed. Turn off one burner for indirect cooking and lower other to medium.

Place ribs in a large baking dish and pour the juice mixture over the ribs. Cover tightly and place in over or on the indirect heat on the grill. Close and cook for one hour. After one hour, remove the ribs, discard juices and solids, and reserve ribs until ready to finish on the grill. This can all be done up to 3 days in advance.

Guava Glaze

Combine jelly, brown sugar, lime juice, vinegar, cumin, and salt in a small saucepan. Place over high heat and bring to boil stirring constantly. Reduce heat to simmer and cook for about 15 minutes uncovered stirring occasionally. Let cool to room temperature. Divide the mixture so that half the glaze can be used to baste and the other half for swerving at the table.

Preheat grill and place ribs meat side down on the grill over direct heat. Close lid and cook for about 5 minutes. Turn ribs over and grill for another

5 minutes. Flip one more time and brush generously with the guava glaze.

Cook for 2 - 3 minutes turn over again and brush the other side with glaze. Cook 2 -3 minutes more and transfer to platter. Cut into individual ribs if desired.

Ribs are awesome when served with smashed and sautéed plantain. Just slice the fruit in ¾ inch pieces, flatten them slightly with palm of your hand, and cook in canola oil or butter.

Nachos de Platano

Description

Plantain nachos, a nice twist on traditional nachos.

Ingredients

oil for frying
plantain, thinly sliced
chicken breast, sliced
onions, chopped
green, red and yellow bell peppers, sliced or chopped
garlic
your choice of spices: cumin, oregano, cayenne, etc
Monterey jack cheese (shredded)

Directions

1. Stir fry the onions, bell peppers, garlic and spices until tender.
2. Fry the plantain slices in oil until golden and crisp.
3. Layer the bottom of a pie or casserole dish with the fried plantain "chips".
4. Layer the sliced chicken breast cover with the stir-fried vegetables and spices.
5. Add some shredded jack cheese and broil until the cheese just melts.

Ingredients

oil for frying
plantain, thinly sliced
chicken breast, sliced
onions, chopped
green, red and yellow bell peppers, sliced or chopped
garlic
your choice of spices: cumin, oregano, cayenne, etc
Monterey jack cheese (shredded)

Directions

1. Stir fry the onions, bell peppers, garlic and spices until tender.
2. Fry the plantain slices in oil until golden and crisp.

3. Layer the bottom of a pie or casserole dish with the fried plantain "chips".
4. Layer the sliced chicken breast cover with the stir-fried vegetables and spices.
5. Add some shredded jack cheese and broil until the cheese just melts.

Pan Frito

Ingredients

¼ cup olive oil for sautéing
3 cloves garlic, crushed with a pinch of salt
1 tablespoon chopped fresh parsley
1 loaf Cuban bread sliced into one-inch thick slices (you may substitute French bread)
lemon juice to taste
freshly grated Parmesan cheese (optional)

Directions
1. Slice the bread into one-inch slices.
2. Place the rounds on a cutting board and use a heavy frying pan or bacon press to compress them slightly.
3. Heat the oil in a large sauté pan.
4. Toss in the crushed garlic and parsley and sauté for one minute only, stirring constantly.
5. Add the bread and sauté over medium heat until the bread is browned on both sides.
6. Just before removing the toast from the pan, sprinkle the slices with a little fresh lemon juice.
7. Serve immediately.

Directions
1. Slice the bread into one-inch slices.
2. Place the rounds on a cutting board and use a heavy frying pan or bacon press to compress them slightly.
3. Heat the oil in a large sauté pan.
4. Toss in the crushed garlic and parsley and sauté for one minute only, stirring constantly.
5. Add the bread and sauté over medium heat until the bread is browned on both sides.
6. Just before removing the toast from the pan, sprinkle the slices with a little fresh lemon juice.
7. Serve immediately.

Cuban Cod and Black Bean Salad

Ingredients

¾ lb. firm white fillets (cod, rockfish, snapper, orange roughy, lingcod, pike)

vegetable cooking spray

1 clove garlic; minced

1 tbsp. + 4 tsp lime juice; divided

¼ cup vegetable oil

½ tsp ground cumin

¼ tsp red pepper flakes or cayenne pepper

¼ tsp salt

1 can black beans (15 oz can) - drained and rinsed

1 large orange

4 cups torn romaine lettuce

Directions

1. Place in even layer (tucking under thin ends) on broiler pan coated with vegetable cooking spray.
2. Combine garlic and 2 teaspoons lime juice; spread on.
3. Broil about 4 inches from heat about 5 minutes or until just flakes when tested with a fork.
4. Transfer to a dish and let cool 10 minutes.
5. Combine oil, remaining 1 tablespoon and 2 teaspoons lime juice, cumin, pepper flakes and salt in a small jar.
6. Shake well and pour 1 tablespoon over.
7. Meanwhile, peel orange, cut into ½-inch slices and separate into segments.
8. Combine with black beams and remaining dressing.
9. Drain, break into large chunks and remove any bones.
10. Add to orange mixture and toss gently.
11. Cover and refrigerate 2 hours or up to 24 hours.
12. Serve over romaine.

Cuban Lentil Salad
with Spicy Vinaigrette

Ingredients

6 cups water

IMG 1713-1-300x225

1½ tbsp. coarse sea salt

1½ cups lentils rinsed, picked over

5 tbsp. extra-virgin olive oil

4 large garlic cloves cut into slivers

½ tsp ground cumin

½ tsp ground coriander
1 tsp cayenne pepper
1 tsp salt
¼ cup white wine vinegar
4 green onions, white, light green parts sliced thin diagonal
¼ cup finely-diced jícama
fresh parsley sprigs for garnish
lemon wedges for garnish

Directions

1. In a large pot, bring the water to a boil and add the salt.
2. Add the lentils, reduce the heat to low, and cook covered for 30 minutes.
3. The lentils should be tender but not mushy.
4. Take care not to overcook them or they can fall apart.
5. While the lentils are cooking, in a medium skillet, heat 1 tablespoon of the olive oil over medium-low heat.
6. Add the garlic and cook gently for 5 to 6 minutes, or until softened and just slightly golden.
7. Do not allow to brown.
8. Remove from the heat and add the cumin, coriander, cayenne, and salt.
9. Stir in the vinegar and then transfer the mixture to a large serving bowl.
10. Drain the lentils in a colander, and immediately transfer them to the bowl.
11. Toss together until the lentils are evenly coated with the dressing, then drizzle the remaining 4 tablespoons of olive oil over the top and toss again just to mix.
12. Cool to room temperature, stir in the scallions and jícama, and serve immediately, or refrigerate for 1 or 2 hours, to allow the flavors to marry.
13. Garnish with sprigs of parsley and lemon wedges.

Pan Frito

Ingredients

¼ cup olive oil for sautéing
3 cloves garlic, crushed with a pinch of salt
1 tablespoon chopped fresh parsley
1 loaf Cuban bread sliced into one-inch thick slices (you may substitute French bread)
lemon juice to taste
freshly grated Parmesan cheese (optional)

Directions

1. Slice the bread into one-inch slices.
2. Place the rounds on a cutting board and use a heavy frying pan or bacon press to compress them slightly.
3. Heat the oil in a large sauté pan.
4. Toss in the crushed garlic and parsley and sauté for one minute only, stirring constantly.
5. Add the bread and sauté over medium heat until the bread is browned on both sides.
6. Just before removing the toast from the pan, sprinkle the slices with a little fresh lemon juice.
7. Serve immediately.

Cuban Picadillo

Ingredients

1 lb. ground meat
1 large onion, chopped
2 – 3 garlic cloves, chopped
1 small can tomato sauce
¼ cup dry white wine
pimento-stuffed olives
raisins
salt and pepper to taste

Directions

1. In a large skillet, brown the ground meat, onions and garlic, pouring out any excess fat.
2. Reduce the heat to medium low and add the tomato sauce and white wine.
3. While that simmers, chop up the olives and add them to the meat mixture.
4. Add the raisins and adjust the seasonings.
5. Serve over fluffy, white rice.

Boniatos Fritos

Description

Fried sweet potato rounds. Makes 4 to 6 servings

Ingredients

Vegetable or peanut oil for frying
4 med Boniatos or American sweet potatoes or yams, peeled and cut into ¼-inch rounds
salt to taste

Directions

1. In a large skillet over medium-high heat, heat ½ inch of oil to 375 °F, or until a piece of potato sizzles when it touches the oil.
2. Add as many potato rounds as will fit in a single layer, reduce the heat to medium, and fry until golden on both sides, 4 to 5 minutes, turning with a slotted spoon.

3. Drain on a paper-towel-lined platter, sprinkle with salt, and serve hot.
4. If you are frying large quantities, keep them warm in a 200 °F oven until all are done.

Torticas de Moron

Ingredients

3 cups all-purpose flour
1 cup sugar
1½ tsp grated lime zest
1 cup shortening

Directions

1. Preheat oven to 350°F.
2. Mix shortening and sugar.
3. Add flour one tablespoon at a time making sure to mix well with each addition.
4. Add the lime zest and mix thoroughly.
5. Roll out the dough.
6. Cut into 2" diameter circles and shape into patties using your hands.
7. Place on cookie sheet covered with parchment paper and bake for 20 to 25 minutes.

Cuban Pork and Chickpea Soup

Ingredients

vegetable cooking spray
1-pound pork tenderloin
1 teaspoon olive oil
¾ cup onion, diced
½ cup burgundy or other dry red wine
1 cup diced red bell pepper
⅓ cup sliced celery
2 tablespoons minced fresh jalapeno pepper
¼ teaspoon salt
2 (10½-ounce) cans low-sodium chicken broth
1 (15-ounce) can chickpeas, drained
6 cloves garlic, minced

Directions

1. Trim any fat from the tenderloin, then cut into ½-inch cubes.
2. Coat a large pot or Dutch oven with cooking spray.
3. Add oil and place over medium-high heat, when hot, add the pork and cook for about 3 minutes or until brown.
4. Then add the onions and wine and cook for another few minutes.
5. Add the red bell pepper and remaining ingredients; bring to a boil.
6. Cover, reduce heat, and let simmer for 30 minutes, stirring occasionally.

Mariquitas de Platanos

Description

Green plantain chips - Makes 2 to 2½ cups of chips

Ingredients

1. 2 large green plantains, peeled and cut into paper-thin slices
2. peanut or vegetable oil for deep frying
3. salt to taste

Directions

1. Place the plantain slices in a bowl, cover them with cold water, and soak 30 minutes (if you are frying right away, you do not need to soak in water).
2. Drain the slices and pat dry with paper towels.
3. In a frying pan or deep fryer over medium-high heat, heat 2 to 3 inches of oil to 375°F, or until a slice of plantain sizzles when it touches the oil, and fry the plantain chips a handful at a time, turning them with a slotted spoon until they are golden brown and crisp.
4. Do not fry too many chips at once, or the oil temperature will fall and the chips will be soggy rather than crisp.
5. Drain on a paper-towel-lined platter, transfer to a serving bowl, sprinkle with salt, and serve hot.

Beef Stew with Cuban Coffee Gravy

Ingredients

1 lb. boned rump roast
¼ tsp salt
¼ tsp coarsely ground black pepper
1½ cup strong brewed coffee
1 cup no-salt-added beef broth
½ cup finely chopped onion
⅓ cup dry red wine
2 garlic cloves minced
1 cup diced peeled taro root or 1 cup diced peeled potato
1 cup sliced mushrooms
¼ cup whole pitted dates chopped
1 tbsp. capers
2 cup hot cooked long-grain rice
½ cup shredded chayote or yellow squash

Directions

1. Trim fat from beef, and cut into 1-inch cubes. Sprinkle with salt and pepper. Heat a large saucepan over medium-high heat. Add beef, and cook 5 minutes or until browned. Add coffee and next 4 ingredients (coffee through garlic), and bring to a boil. Cover, reduce heat, and simmer 45 minutes.
2. Add taro, mushrooms, dates, and capers; bring to a boil. Cover, reduce heat, and simmer 20 minutes. Serve over rice; top with chayote.

Notes

1. Serving size and accompaniment:1¼ cups stew, ½ cup rice, and 2 tablespoons chayote
2. Suggested wine: Cabernet Sauvignon
3. To make strong coffee, you can skip the brewing process by mixing a tablespoon of instant espresso granules with 1½ cups of hot water.

(Beef Stew with Cuban Coffee , 2017)

Rum

My first Mojito in Cuba

(Cuban Rum, 2017)

The rum from Cuba has a worldwide reputation.

Rum is produced by fermenting and distilling molasses or honey or sugarcane juice. The clear liquid is then usually aged in oak barrels. Light rums are usually used in cocktails while darker rums are consumed over ice.

The Royal Navy once mixed rum with water or beer to make grog.

Classic Rum Cocktails

Mojito Recipe
Rum and mint cocktail

Mojito is a traditional Cuban blend, **a rum and mint cocktail**, invented in Cuba, which became trendy in the United States during the late 1890s. Ernest

Hemingway was partial to the Mojitos at La Bodeguita del Medio in Havana, Cuba, his recipe had no sugar. This is how they prepare Mojito cocktails at **La** *Bodeguita del Medio:*

1 teaspoon of sugar
¼ ounce fresh lime juice,
2 mint sprigs
Add 1½ oz. white Cuban rum to 2 oz. soda water and 4 crushed ice cubes.
Stir well and garnish with a sprig of mint.

Daiquiri Recipe

Daiquiri is a family of Cuban cocktails whose main ingredients are rum and lime juice. Daiquiri is also the name of a beach near Santiago de Cuba, and an iron mine in that area. It is said that an American named Jennings Cox, an engineer who worked in the mine, invented the drink when he ran out of gin while entertaining guests. Daiquiri Natural is the basic mix, that serves as the starting point to the more complex cocktails of the family:

1.3 oz. light-dry Cuban rum
0.7 oz. lime juice
1 teaspoon sugar
crushed ice
Mix the ingredients in a shaker and serve.

Cuba Libre Recipe

The Cuba Libre is a Cuban cocktail made of:

3 ounces cola
Lime wedge
1-ounce rum

Preparation:

Rub the rim of a highball glass with lime.

Fill with ice.

Add rum and fill with cola.

Drop in the lime squeeze.

Havana Special Recipe

An all-time classic cocktail from Havana Cuba: Blend in the shaker:
5 cl Pineapple juice
5 cl Havana Club Anejo Blanco
A dash of Maraschino
Crushed ice
Shake well and strain into a cocktail glass.

Havana Club Rum

Exists in different versions:
3 years old Havana Club (Anejo Blanco)
5 years old Havana Club (Anejo oro)
7 years old Havana Club (Anejo 7 anos)
Anejo Especial
Havana Club 15 years old – Grand Reserva

Cuban Cigars

Havana cigars are famous for their quality and taste but what do Cubans smoke?

Partagas Factory Related pages (Cuban Cigars, 2016):

Cigars are made in Cuba with tobacco grown in the Pinar Valley. The climate of the valley creates the leaf of the plant that is superb for producing the fine Cuban Cigars treasured though out the world. The only other region of the world that produces the types of leaves used to make Cuban like Cigars is in the Connecticut Tobacco Valley where I live. Our nets create the microclimate found in the Pinar Valley.

Fidel Castro's favorite cigar was the Cuban Cohiba cigar.

Counterfeit cigars have been produced in the Dominican Republi,c so buyer beware.

The anatomy of a cigar

The <u>head</u> is the end you put in your mouth. It should be sealed off and should be cut with a sharp knife or "guillotine" to allow the smoke to flow through the cigar.

The word cohiba derives from the Taíno word meaning tobacco. Cohiba is a brand of cigar produced by the Cuban Government and in the Dominican Republic for the General Cigar Company in Evansville, Indiana.

The <u>foot</u> is the end that you light with the piece of cedar wood found in the tube.

The <u>filler</u> inside is usually a blend of dried and fermented tobacco. The most important part of the cigar is the wrapper outside. It is usually made from three leaves varying in color from light to dark. This portion of the cigar creates the flavor.

Some things to keep in mind when selecting a quality cigar.

"As a general rule Cuban cigars burn slowly and produce a grey ash."

First: The cigar should be solid but soft to the touch.

Second: The aroma of the cigar should be pleasant and rich.

Romeo y Julieta a brand of premium cigars produced by the Cuban Government and in the Dominican Republic by a division of Imperial Tobacco.

Third: the cigar should be solid but not dry. Humidors are used to keep the moisture content consistent without getting the cigar moldy. Wrappers produced in Connecticut have been stored for up to fifty years back to the time when my grandfather worked as a tobacco broker.

Counterfeit Cigars

0-1 View inside the Partagas Tobacco Factory near the Capitolio in Central Havana.

Counterfeit Cuban cigars are a big industry in the Caribbean as well as in Cuba. Basically, you should only buy Cuban cigars from a government-licensed merchants and the box or tub should have the seal from the Cuban

Government. Those without the seal are most certainly guaranteed to be a counterfeit of some kind.

Importation of Cuban Tobacco into the United States

The ban on the importation into the United States of Cuban cigars and other tobacco products from the island of Cuba has been lifted since 2014 although there is a limit on the quantity that you can bring back to the United States.

Note: Read the complete regulations and laws on Cuba sanctions (www.treas.gov) Cuban tobacco update (Source: US Department of the Treasury)

Interesting Fact: The cedar sheet in a tube or box of cigars is used to light your cigar. Tear off a strip, then light it and use the lit piece of cedar to light your cigar. Matches and cigarette lighters give the cigar a bad flavor.

Bibliography

(n.d.). Retrieved from http://www.treasury.gov/resourceenter/sanctions/Programs/Documents/31cfr515new. pdf

Range of Cuban Missiles. (1962, 10 16). Retrieved from The National Security Archives: http://nsarchive.gwu.edu/nsa/cuba_mis_cri/17.jpg

10 Incredible Facts Sense of Smell. (2014). Retrieved from Everyday Health: http://www.everydayhealth.com/news/incredible-facts-about-your-sense-smell/

20 dishes everyone should try in Cuba. (2017). Retrieved from The Business: http://www.the-leader.com/article/20150424/BUSINESS/304249974

20 Facts Sense Smell. (2016). Retrieved from UK Mirror Lifestyle Magazine: http://www.mirror.co.uk/lifestyle/health/20-fascinating-facts-sense-smell-1977351

(2016, 02 26). Retrieved from Word Reference: http://wordrefernce.com/tamale

(2016). Retrieved from Chiapas Tamale: http://en.wikipedia.org/ChiapasTamale2.JPG

A Taste of Cuba. (2017). Retrieved from Medianoche: https://en.wikipedia.org/wiki/Medianoche

Beef Stew with Cuban Coffee . (2017). Retrieved from Recipes Wikia: http://recipes.wikia.com/wiki/Beef_Stew_with_Cuban_Coffee_Gravy

Best Food in Cuba. (2016). Retrieved from INSIDER: http://www.thisisinsider.com/best-food-in-cuba-2016-12

Best Food in Cuba. (2016). Retrieved from UK Business Insider: http://uk.businessinsider.com/best-food-in-cuba-2016-12?op=1

Bruyere, D. (2008, 06 07). *Trinidad.* Retrieved from Plaza Mayor and Iglesia y Convento de San Francisco: https://en.wikipedia.org

Caayo Largo. (2017). Retrieved from Vacation Cuba: https://www.vacuba.com/destinations/Cayo%20Largo

Cannon, T. (1981). *Frank País and the Underground Movement in the cities.* Retrieved from historyofcuba.com

Cannon, T. (2006, 05 21). *Who was Frank Pais?* Retrieved from History of Cuba: historyofcuba.com

Castro, L. (2011). Latin Grilling. In L. Castro. Ten Speed Press, a division of Random House, Inc.

Chisholm, H. (1911). Gibara. In *Encyclopædia Britannica.* Cambridge University Press.

158

Churros. (2016). Retrieved from https://en.wikipedia.org

CIA Library. (2017). Retrieved from CIA World Fact Book: https://www.cia.gov/library/publications/the-world-factbook/fields/2081.html

Classic Cuban Midnight (Medianoche) Sandwich Recipe. (2017). Retrieved from Spark People: https://recipes.sparkpeople.com/recipe-detail.asp?recipe=656334

Coconut and Rum Flan - Flan de Coco. (2017). Retrieved from I Cuban: https://icuban.com/food/flan_de_coco.html

Colon Cemetary. (2017). Retrieved from La Habana, Cuba: http://www.interment.net/data/cuba/lahabana/colon/index.htm

Cooking Channel TV. (2016). Retrieved from http://www.cookingchanneltv.com/recipes/croquetas-de-jamon-y-queso.html

Croquettes. (2016). Retrieved from http://www.jamesbeard.org/blog/eat-word-croquettes

Cuba Tourism. (2016). Retrieved from National Office of Tourist Information: http://www.infotur.cu/mapas.aspx

Cuba Tourism Portal. (n.d.). Retrieved from Cuba Tourism Portal: http://www.cubatravel.cu/en/

Cuban Cigars. (2016). Retrieved from Havana Guide: http://www.havana-guide.com/havana-cigars.html

Cuban Food. (2016). Retrieved from Havana Guide: http://www.havana-guide.com/cuba-food.html

Cuban Food. (2017). Retrieved from Havana Guide: http://www.havana-guide.com/cuba-food.html

Cuban Rum. (2017). Retrieved from Havana Guide: http://www.havana-guide.com/cuban-rum.html

Department of Treasury, Office of Foreign Assets Control, Cuban Assets Control Regulations. (2016). Retrieved from https://www.treasury.gov/resource-center/sanctions/Programs/Pages/cuba.aspx

Discover Cuba. (2017). Retrieved from Chamber Explorations: http://www.chamberexplorations.com/destinations/cuba.php

Ernest Hemingway's Home in Cuba. (2015). Retrieved from Hemingway's Cuba: http://www.hemingwaycuba.com/finca-la-vigia.html

FCC: FAQs for Travelers to Cuba. (2016). Retrieved from https://www.fcc.gov/consumers/guides/telecommunications-faqs-travelers-cuba

Florida bank issues first U.S. credit card for use in Cuba. (2016, 06 14). Retrieved from The Denver Post:

http://www.denverpost.com/2016/06/14/ florida-bank-issues-first-us-credit-card-for-use-in-cuba/

Frank, S. M. (2017, January 3). Las Vegas Journal Review. *Cuans hopeful despite uncertainty*, p. 14A.

Free Health Care? (2011). Retrieved from http://www.therealcuba.com/?page_id=77

Free Healthcare? (2011). Retrieved from The Real Cuba: http://www.therealcuba.com/?page_id=77

Frita. (2018). Retrieved from Wikipedia: https://en.wikipedia.org

Gifts - Cuba Forum. (2017). Retrieved from Trip Advisor: https://www.tripadvisor.com/ShowTopic-g147270-i91-k10279102-Gifts-Cuba.html

Havana. (2017). Retrieved from Wikipedia: https://en.wikipedia.org/wiki/Havana

Havana Cuba the Lost Island. (2011). Retrieved from memographer.com: http://memographer.com/2011/10/havana-cuba-the-lost-island/

Havana Cuba Tours. (2017). Retrieved from Travel Store: https://www.travelstore.com/travel-journals/touring-havana-cuba

Health Information for Travelers to Cuba. (2016). Retrieved from http://wwwnc.cdc.gov/travel/destinations/traveler/none/cuba

Hoyer, D. a. (2008). Tamales. In D. a. Hoyer. Gibbs Smith.

Ignacio Maza, V. -S. (2015).

Legal Travel to Cuba. (2017). Retrieved from Travel to Cuba: http://www.cuba-travel.com/how-to-travel-to-cuba-from-us-legally

NSA Archives. (1962). Retrieved from http://nsarchive.gwu.edu/nsa/cuba_mis_cri/photos.htm

NSA|CSS - Cuban Missile Crisis. (1960-64). Retrieved from https://www.nsa.gov/news-features/declassified-documents/cuban-missile-crisis/1960.shtml

Ordering Wine. (2014). Retrieved from http://www.businessinsider.com/what-not-to-do-when-ordering-wine-2013-12

Photo courtesy of Cuba Tourism. (2016).

Photo courtesy of Fathom Cruise Line. (2016).

Photo courtesy of Linda Safier. (2016). Travel Professional.

Pinar del Rio. (2017). Retrieved from Cuba Explorer: https://cubaexplorer.com/pinar-del-rio/

Plaza de la Revolución. (2017). Retrieved from Wikipedia: https://en.wikipedia.org/wiki/Plaza_de_la_Revoluci%C3%B3n

Raichlen, S. (1993). Miami Spice: the New Florida Cuisine. In S. Raichlen. Workman Publishing.

Ramekin. (2016). Retrieved from https://en.wikipedia.org/wiki/Ramekin

Red paella with mussels.jpg. (2017). Retrieved from https://en.wikipedia.org

Santiago de Cuba. (2017). Retrieved from Wikipedia: https://en.wikipedia.org/wiki/Santiago_de_Cuba

Sense of Smell. (2013). Retrieved from http://www.ncbi.nlm.nih.gov/pubmedhealth/PMHT0025081/

Sense of Taste. (2012). Retrieved from http://www.ncbi.nlm.nih.gov/pubmedhealth/PMH0072592/

Shaoruzhu.jpg. (2017). Retrieved from Lechon asado: http://en.wikipedia.org

Tamales. (2017). Retrieved from Tamales Lilianas: http://www.tamaleslilianas.co/AboutUs.html

Telecommunications FAQs for Travelers to Cuba. (2016, 10 31). Retrieved from FCC.gov: https://transition.fcc.gov/cgb/consumerfacts/cuba-travel-faqs.pdf

The National Security Archive. (1962, 11 9). Retrieved from Nuclear warheads in Luna: http://nsarchive.gwu.edu/nsa/cuba_mis_cri/46.jpg

Travants. (2015). *Visiting Cuba As An American: Get the Facts.* Retrieved from Travants Destination LowDown - Cuba Travel Specialists: http://www.travants.com/cubainfo.php

Tropicana Show Havanna. (2017). Retrieved from Erlebe Kuba Reisen: http://www.erlebe-kuba.de/osh/de/html/detail/cuba/0,69,.html

UNESCO: Alejandro de Humboldt National Park. (2016). Retrieved from http://whc.unesco.org/en/list/839

UNESCO: Archaeological Landscape of the First Coffee Plantations in the South-East of Cuba. (2016). Retrieved from http://whc.unesco.org/en/list/1008

UNESCO: Desembarco del Granma National Park. (n.d.). Retrieved from http://whc.unesco.org/en/list/889

UNESCO: Historic Centre of Camagüey. (2016). Retrieved from http://whc.unesco.org/en/list/1270

UNESCO: Old Havana and its Fortifications. (2016). Retrieved from UNESCO: http://whc.unesco.org/en/list/204

UNESCO: San Pedro de la Roca Castle, Santiago de Cuba. (2016). Retrieved from http://whc.unesco.org/en/list/841

UNESCO: Trinidad and the Valley de los Ingenios. (2016). Retrieved from http://whc.unesco.org/en/list/460

UNESCO: Trinidad, Cuba. (2016). Retrieved from http://www.ovpm.org/en/cuba/trinidad

UNESCO: Urban Historic Centre of Cienfuegos. (2016). Retrieved from http://whc.unesco.org/en/list/1202

UNESCO: Viñales (Cuba). (2016). Retrieved from http://whc.unesco.org/archive/advisory_body_evaluation/840.pdf

UNESCO: Viñales Valley. (2016). Retrieved from http://whc.unesco.org/en/list/840

Vaca frita at cuba nyc.jpg. (2016). Retrieved from Wikipedia Photo: https://en.wikipedia.org/Vaca frita at cuba nyc.jpg

Walter, N. (2008). *Habits of Empire, A History of American Expansion.* Retrieved from http://www.abmc.gov/memorials/memorials/sst.php

Webmaster. (2017). *Destinations Pinar-del-Rio.* Retrieved from Cuba Travel: http://www.cubatravel.cu/en/Destinations/Pinar-del-Rio

INTERACTIVE RESOURCES

Website http://www.CruiseWithBruce.com
Blog http://Blog.CruiseWithBruce.com
Quarterly Sweepstakes http://Win.CruiseWithBruce.com
Contact http://VirtualLuxury.net/contact
Facebook http://www.facebook.com/cruiseradionetwork
http://www.facebook.com/cruisewithbruce
http://www.facebook.com/groups/BruceOliverTV
Twitter http://www.twitter.com/BruceOliverCT
YouTube http://www.youtube.com/cruisewithbruce
Blog Talk Radio
http://www.blogtalkradio.com/cruisewithbruce/podcast
iTunes https://itunes.apple.com/us/podcast/food-wine-art-theme-based/id400027948?mt=2
TuneIn Radio
http://tunein.com/radio/Cruise-with-Bruce-p382915/
Instagram https://instagram.com/bruceoliverct/
Pinterest https://www.pinterest.com/cruisewithbruce/
Scratch and Sniff Travel™ http://ScratchAndSniffTravel.com
Bruce Oliver, Scent-sational Traveler™
http://scentsationaltraveler.com/
Scent-Sational Travel™ Books
http://ScentsationalTravelBooks.com
Promotions http://Promotions.CruiseWithBruce.com
Yelp https://www.yelp.com/biz/virtual-luxury-network-cruise-with-bruce-enterprises-greenwich
Bruce Oliver TV http://BruceOliverTV
Smart TV Network http://SmartTVtraveler.com
Travel Coloring Books http://TravelingColoringBooks.com

INDEX

Win Sweepstakes

Scan the QR Code above to enter Signature Travel Network's Quarterly Sweepstakes.

http://Win.CruiseWithBruce.com

Every quarter we award an all-inclusive vacation to one lucky winner.

Scan the QR Code above to get a quarterly subscription to a 68-page Travel Magazine

http://Win.CruiseWithBruce.com

Enter all of the information that is requested and be sure to click on email notifications.

About Bruce Oliver – *This book is an introduction to the Sensational Travel & Food Series and the Traveling Coloring Books.*

Bruce Oliver, native of Enfield, CT spends winters in Orlando or Las Vegas. He has traveled to over 49 states, 56 countries and 6 continents. Bruce's paternal great grandparents immigrated to the U.S. from the London (Enfield) England in the 1800's to settle on the country road that is now known as Oliver Road, Enfield, Connecticut. His paternal great grandparents are also from Italy. His maternal grandfather walked from his home near Prague when he was nine years old to take a boat to America from Great Britain. Quite a feat fo r a nine-year old.

Bruce has a passion for global travel and photography.

He's the recipient of the Travel Weekly Silver Magellan Award for individuals in the travel industry and was awarded the 2014 Best of Enfield Cruise Agents. He's a member of OASIS Agent and the Signature Travel Network.

Bruce has certification with the Cruise Line Industry Association (CLIA) and has credentials from the International Air Transport Association (IATA). He is a Luxury Travel Specialist and has "destination specialist" certifications from all over the world as well as a close working relationship with most the cruise lines and travel operators. He is a Level 2 Member of the United Nations Educational, Scientific, and Cultural Organization (AKA - UNESCO): World Heritage Convention.

He also has **travel photographer** press credentials from the **National Press Association** and the **ITWPA**. He is a Professional Photographer registered with the International VR Photography Association (IVRPA) specializing in 360° Virtual Tours. He's listed as a **Charter Member of the Library of Congress** and the **Microsoft Alumni Association**.

He's the recipient of many honors and awards in his community and higher education. In 1989, he graduated with a MBA from the University of Hartford. Bruce is listed in **MARQUIS: Who's Who in America, Who's Who in the World** and **Who's Who in American Education**. Bruce has been a member of the National Eagle Scouts Association since 1967 and is a Vigil Honor Member in BSA's: Order of the Arrow. While attending high school, he was awarded the DeKalb Agricultural Accomplishment Award and the Connecticut State Farmer Degree from the Future Farmers of America.

For more books on travel please visit:

http://SensationalTravelBooks.com

*Please write a **Review on Amazon** for this book. I am always interested in getting feedback and would love to hear what you would like me to include in the next edition. Thanks, Bruce*

http://Amazon.com/author/bruceoliver

———————————————

86334537R00096

Made in the USA
Columbia, SC
12 January 2018